Hold the Oxo!

Hold the Oxo!

MARION FARGEY BROOKER

A Teenage Soldier Writes Home

DUNDURN
TORONTO

Editor: Allison Hirst
Design: Courtney Horner
Printer: Marquis

Library and Archives Canada Cataloguing in Publication

Brooker, Marion 1932-
        Hold the Oxo! : a teenage soldier writes home / written by Marion Fargey Brooker.

Includes bibliographical references and index.
Issued also in electronic formats.
ISBN 978-1-55488-870-2

        1. Fargey, James, 1897-1916. 2. Soldiers--Canada--Biography--Juvenile literature. 3. World War, 1914-1918--Canada--Biography--Juvenile literature. 4. Soldiers--Canada--Correspondence--Juvenile literature.
5. World War, 1914-1918--Personal narratives, Canadian--Juvenile literature.
I. Title.

D640.B76 2011   j940.4'8171   C2011-901918-3

1   2   3   4   5   15   14   13   12   11

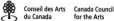 Canada ONTARIO ARTS COUNCIL / CONSEIL DES ARTS DE L'ONTARIO

We acknowledge the support of the **Canada Council for the Arts** and the **Ontario Arts Council** for our publishing program. We also acknowledge the financial support of the **Government of Canada** through the **Canada Book Fund** and **Livres Canada Books**, and the **Government of Ontario** through the **Ontario Book Publishing Tax Credit** and the **Ontario Media Development Corporation**.

Care has been taken to trace the ownership of copyright material used in this book. The author and the publisher welcome any information enabling them to rectify any references or credits in subsequent editions.

J. Kirk Howard, President

Printed and bound in Canada.
www.dundurn.com

Unless specified, all images are from the author's collection.
Front cover image: The young soldier, James Henderson Fargey, date unknown.
Back cover image: Jim (front) and two hometown friends, Arthur Abbis (rear) and Leslie Smith (middle), board the train for Winnipeg, July 21, 1915.
Page 5: The box, decorated by Jim's mother, in which his letters have been kept for close to a century.

Dundurn
3 Church Street, Suite 500
Toronto, Ontario, Canada
M5E 1M2

Gazelle Book Services Limited
White Cross Mills
High Town, Lancaster, England
LA1 4XS

Dundurn
2250 Military Road
Tonawanda, NY
U.S.A. 14150

*For Jim
and all who serve our country*

CONTENTS

Preface 9

Acknowledgements 13

Glossary 15

Introduction 19

1 Three Cheers — We're at War! 27

2 Why Are You Going? 31

3 You're in the Army Now! 35

4 Reality 45

5 Ypres Salient 49

6 In the Trenches 53

7 Surprise Weapons 63

8 A Day in the Life 77

9	Battle of the Somme	89
10	Women in War — The Bluebirds	107
11	Wounded	111
12	Eleventh Month, Eleventh Day, Eleventh Hour	123
	Timeline	129
	Resources	135
	Index	137

PREFACE

June 17, 1916, near Ypres, Belgium

Canadian mail comes Thursday and Sunday. I know when your letters don't come there is something wrong with the mail as I know they are written.

P.S. I am reading over a few of your old letters. I keep your last two or three as I cannot carry them all around.

His letters home are not ones to which you would spare a second glance. The early ones are written on crested paper with pen and ink; the later ones are on rough lined paper, written with a pencil in need of sharpening. Sometimes the youthful scrawl wanders from between the lines — letters written by candlelight from the floor of a tent. Some are long letters; others are only a sentence or two. And some are just short notes from the front line written on cards.

They would not have rated an A grade in school for composition or content. The early letters speak of night training, of the Lee Enfield rifle versus the Ross, Christmas dinners that don't measure up to the home-cooked ones he remembers, and of parades and more parades. They speak of life back home, of the lack of ice in England for skating, of being quarantined for measles, of the socks he received that had been knit by his sister. And when the letters begin to arrive from the battlefields

Armly Leeds
Nov 17th/15

POST WR &S CARD
RELIABLE · SERIES

FOR CORRESPONDENCE.

Dear Sister,
I am spending my holiday at Leeds with Arthur. Am having a fine time. I am sending a piece of music home to you to-day. It is a very popular piece here. We are going back to camp to-morrow. Tell Mother I will write her as soon as I get back to camp. Excuse poor, as the pen is very poor. I snowed here yesterday. It is nearly all gone.

FOR ADDRESS ONLY.

Miss A. Fargey.
Belmont
Manitoba
Canada.

An early crested letter written to his mother (opposite) and a postcard for his sister (above), both sent from England during Jim's training.

of France and Belgium, from Ypres and the Somme, they turn their attention, not to the battles, but to the comfort of the straw in the barn in which the soldiers are billeted, the scarcity of men in France and Belgium to help with the harvest (leaving it to be done by women and old men), the fine French horses, or the luxury of having porridge for breakfast.

Yet these letters, folded and tied carefully, have rested for more than 90 years beneath the lid of the shoebox my grandmother decorated. The creamy velvet has turned sepia and is stained with the oil from many fingers, the corners of the box loosened and warped.

HOLD THE OXO!

Bramshott Camp
Oct 22nd /15

Dear Mother,
Well here we are been two days in camp and a little more settled than we were a day ago. We spent yesterday in cleaning up our rooms and they feel a little better now. All of us are in the same room now. The first night we landed here we had any mattress and only one blanket and had not any fire in the stove. Yesterday we got new mattresses and filled them with fresh straw and got an extra blanket.

We are not sure whether we are going to France or not. The officers do not know whether we are going to or not. We went down to a place called Haselmea last night about three miles off for a good meal but when we got down there all the stores were closed on account of a half holiday; so we took in to another town to-night the other direction and got a good supper of bacon and eggs. It has been raining nearly all

These are not just any letters. They are the letters of a 17-year-old boy, sent home to his mother, his father, his brothers, and his sister. They are the letters of a boy who left a small farming community for the city on July 15, 1915; a boy who joined the 79th Queen's Own Cameron Highlanders, later to become the 43rd in England. Rarely do these letters, especially those to his mother and father, mention the horrors of war — the mud and rats, the lice and the stench of the trenches, the night duty of cutting barbed wire in no man's land. The ones written to older brother Frank are more detailed.

The letters are yellowed now; their edges frayed, not only from age but from the reading and re-reading of them by his family — the family he left behind. Again and again we have read the actual words — and the words not said — the words between the lines.

These are the letters from my 17-year-old uncle, Jim, to his family — my grandparents and my father, my uncle and my aunt. But they could be the letters written by any of the thousands of young men like Jim who joined the "war to end all wars."

ACKNOWLEDGEMENTS

Where does one begin with their appreciation in a story such as this one? With Jim, who served; with my grandmother and grandfather who treasured and saved his letters; with his sister and brothers, who kept his memory alive into the next generation; with my family — immediate and extended — who encouraged and supported my efforts; with my sister and brother, Margaret and Jim, who supplied important details and pictures from family albums; with my husband, Elmer, who travelled with me to the First World War battlefields, monuments, and cemeteries? They all deserve credit for helping me complete this book, and for that I will always be grateful.

For sharing their knowledge, expertise, and time, I am indebted to my writing friends, as well as to Becky Garber-Conrad, Paul Robison, and Fred Sproule, who meticulously read my work and made invaluable suggestions.

My thanks also to the professionals at Dundurn who guided the process of making *Hold the Oxo! A Teenage Soldier Writes Home* a reality — Kirk Howard, Tammy Mavroudi, Margaret Bryant, Shannon Whibbs, Marta Warner, and my editor Allison Hirst.

I also want to acknowledge that the excerpt on page 38 was originally published in *Riding into War: The Memoir of a Horse Transport Driver, 1916–1919*, copyright 2004 by James Robert Johnston. It was reprinted by permission of Goose Lane Editions and The Brigadier Milton F. Gregg VC, Centre for the Study of War and Society.

And finally, the greatest thanks of all must go to all the Canadian men and women who, like Jim, have believed in and served this country. It is in their memory that I dedicate *Hold the Oxo! A Teenage Soldier Writes Home.*

GLOSSARY

Allies: Britain, France, Italy, Russia, the United States, and the countries that fought with them in the First World War.

Aperture: an opening, hole.

Army units: the organization of the British forces during the First World War: the British Forces on the Western Front were divided into four or five **armies** (approximately 4 million [1917] soldiers in the field); an **army** had two or more **corps** (varied, but as many as 120,000); a **corps** contained several **divisions**; a **division** (20,000 men) had three **infantry brigades** plus artillerymen, a medical section, engineers, and pioneers; a **brigade** (4,000 infantry men) had four **battalions** plus engineers, signals, field ambulance, trench mortar unit, and machine-gun unit; a **battalion** consisted of 1,000 men, made up of several **companies** of 200 men, which was then broken into several **platoons** (50 soldiers).

Artillery: big weapons such as cannons and the forces that use them.

Bayonet: a sharp, steel blade attached to the end of a rifle.

Bivouac: to camp.

Bombardment: an attack with heavy artillery.

Box Social: a fundraising dance during which decorated boxes filled with lunches by the women were auctioned off. The donors of the boxes were usually anonymous.

Boches: Germans.

Breastwork: a temporary defence or parapet, usually chest-high.

British Expeditionary Force (B.E.F.): a term used for all British forces on the Western Front.

Bunker: underground shelter, normally made of concrete.

Central Powers: Germany, Austria-Hungary, Turkey, and Bulgaria.

Creeping barrage: an infantry advance behind a line of friendly artillery fire. It was used for the first time at the Battle of the Somme, and later (and more effectively) at Vimy.

Dugout: a space dug underground or in the wall of a trench, often used as an officer's quarters, a gun emplacement, or for added protection of the soldiers from the weather. Sometimes called "funk" holes.

Enfilade: gunfire directed along a line from end to end.

Fritz: an Allied nickname for a German soldier.

Front: front line, where two opposing armies meet.

Gas: chlorine gas was a poisonous gas that smelled like a swimming pool. Mustard gas had a mustard-like odour and a brownish-yellow colour.

Haversack: a large bag for carrying provisions, carried on the back or over the shoulder.

Janes: slang for "girls."

Mess tin: a portable version of a saucepan, intended primarily for boiling but also useful for frying.

Munitions: ammunition.

Outflank: to attack the enemy by moving around the side of their line.

Ox-o (trademark): the trademark for an extract of beef stock, condensed and sold in small cubes for use in cooking or, when mixed with hot water, as a beverage.

Parapets: the side of the trench directly facing the enemy line, often topped with several feet of sandbags for the protection of soldiers.

Parados: the rear of the trench.

Salient: an area of the battlefield that extends into enemy territory and is surrounded on three sides by the enemy. The Ypres Salient encircled the ancient town of Ypres, Belgium.

"That's Jake": slang for "That's okay."

Western Front: front lines between the Allies and the Central Powers in France and Belgium.

INTRODUCTION

My Dear Grandma,

You might call this a thank-you letter. It is in appreciation to you for, so many years ago, saving each of your son's letters — letters that were treasured by his sister and his brothers and have now been read and re-read by his nieces and nephews. Had you looked into the future, could you have dreamed that by saving Jim's letters we would come to know so much about an uncle who died years before we were born?

It is October 1914, and the Patriotic Society in Belmont, Manitoba, is holding a dance and box social to raise money for the war effort. You bend over a shoe box, covering it with cream-coloured velvet, mitering the corners, and gluing them all in place. On the lid you paint a Union Jack, flying high, and inscribe underneath it the date — October 14, 1914. In it you will put the lunch that will be auctioned off at ten o'clock this evening, the lunch break during the dance. Do you even dream as you work on the box that nine months from now it will hold the letters home from your son, Jim, who is now in high school? That fall, both sides in the battle that has just begun overseas believe that the First World War will be over by Christmas.

The tall, handsome young woman decorating the shoe box is not the grandmother I remember. My memory is not one of a young mother raising four children, but of a fragile lady with arthritis confined to a wheelchair. Being the youngest in the family, I was allowed to skip the evening church service, and I remember crawling in behind you in your high mahogany bed, where we would talk or you would read me stories. The smell of wintergreen, the cure-all for arthritis, still brings back those memories.

Only after having children of my own, Grandma, could I understand the heartache of losing a son. I am haunted by the thought of Jim being buried so far away from home, with next to no chance for you to visit his grave. You would be comforted to know that Jim has been visited by and has become a real person to three generations of our family. If I could speak to you of one thing, I would choose to describe to you the cemetery just outside Étaples where he is buried. A large white cross, magnificent in its simplicity, stands as a benediction over the graves. The cemetery slopes gently to the English Channel, where you can look across the water to England. Red poppies do, indeed, sway in the breeze here. A stooped French veteran with a blue beret, an old man now, lovingly tends the graves. We found Jim's. The picture you received of a stark pile of dirt with only a wooden post to identify Jim's resting place has been replaced by a soft-beige granite stone. Summer flowers arch over his name.

I procrastinated in writing Jim's story. I wanted to do justice, not only to Jim but to all who fought. My dilemma: who should tell the story? In the end, I let Jim speak for himself by using excerpts from his letters. However, when I began filling in the background details, of which Jim speaks little in his letters — about life in the trenches and on the battlefields, and the hardships of war — I could often hear Jim's voice saying, "How could you know? You weren't there."

Yes, I have visited the battlefields of Ypres and the Somme, and the Canadian monument at Vimy, touched with my fingers the names of soldiers with no grave that are carved in the Menin Gate and the Thiepval Memorial. I have seen the battlefields of Flanders — lush now — zigzagging grassy trenches, craters no longer filled with the bodies of men and horses, the barbed wire long gone. I have stood surrounded by the trees in Delville Wood and touched the one mutilated tree left standing on its own at the end of the war, its leaves and limbs shredded by artillery fire.

HOLD THE OXO!

LEST WE FORGET

Canadian National Vimy Memorial

This impressive memorial is dedicated to the memory of Canadian Expeditionary Force members killed during the First World War. It also serves as the place of commemoration for First World War Canadian soldiers killed or presumed dead in France who have no known grave. The monument is the centrepiece of a 100-hectare preserved battlefield park that encompasses a portion of the grounds over which the Canadian Corps made their assault during the Battle of Vimy Ridge.

The inscription on the monument reads: TO THE VALOUR OF THEIR/COUNTRYMEN IN THE GREAT WAR/AND IN MEMORY OF THEIR SIXTY THOUSAND DEAD THIS MONUMENT/IS RAISED BY THE PEOPLE OF CANADA.

The sculpture of a sorrowful woman, Canada Bereft, *on the Vimy monument represents Canada — a young nation mourning her dead. The massive sculpture was carved from a single 30-tonne block of stone.*

The memorial was restored over several years and rededicated by Queen Elizabeth II in 2007, the 90th anniversary of the Battle of Vimy Ridge. The site is one of two National Historic Sites of Canada located outside of Canada.

I have walked among the row on row of white gravestones stretching to the horizon at Tyne Cot, near Passchendaele, flowers bending gently now in the summer breeze over the cold granite. I have stood outside the concrete bunker where John McCrae bandaged shattered legs, swabbed gaping wounds, and I have rested in the tiny cemetery outside this dressing station at Essex Farm where McCrae rested one afternoon during a lull in the fighting. He had just lost a friend, and it was here that he wrote:

We are the Dead. Short days ago
We lived, felt dawn, saw sunset glow,
Loved and were loved, and now we lie
In Flanders fields.

But Jim is right. I wasn't there. The countryside today is not the countryside of the First World War. I can only try to imagine it, and my mind cannot comprehend such horror.

Because of censorship and of wanting to protect you all from war's savagery, many of Jim's letters speak, as you know, more of what is happening at home on the farm than on the battlefields of Belgium and France, so I have not used his letters in their entirety.

The letters are Jim's, but his story is that of thousands of young people who joined the fight to put an end to all wars, but sadly did not make it home. It is also about those who returned, scarred physically and emotionally from what they had seen and done.

Hold the Oxo! is the story of day-to-day life in the trenches, in the tunnels, behind the artillery, in the sky, and on the sea. It is the story of the generals who laid the plans and gave the orders, confronted by a war fought from the trenches and tunnels of Flanders and France — a war for which their training had not prepared them.

There are so many questions I would like to ask you and Grandpa if I could. Although Jim entered his correct birthdate as December 1897 on his attestation papers, it seems the officer made a mistake and entered his "apparent age" as 18 years and 7 months. In fact, Jim was only 17 years and 7 months when he joined up. He writes home from England on December 16 of that same year: "P.S. I forgot to mention that I am eighteen today. Little did I think a year ago today that I would be in England." Did you and Grandpa object to his joining so young, and did he go anyway?

John McCrae, poet, physician, and field surgeon in the Canadian Artillery during the First World War.

I wonder why the letters from Staff Nurse Angela N. Sadleir were addressed only to you and not to Grandpa — even the one announcing his death, and the letters of condolence. Was this customary? In an early letter from France, Jim explains why most of his letters are addressed to you, with only a few to Grandpa: "Just a few lines to let you know I'm still alive and thriving well. I've told Mother nearly all the news and I guess her letters are read aloud." Jim's letters to his brother Frank would have been sent to Winnipeg, where Frank was attending college.

HOLD THE OXO!

Although Jim rarely speaks of loneliness or fear in his letters, I cannot help but imagine him lying in the hospital bed in France, a boy far from his farm home. I would like to be able to show you a picture we have of his youngest brother (my dad) beside his grave in 1965. Could Jim have dreamed in that time of slow communication and travel that three generations would be able to visit his grave to remember and honour his and so many of his comrades' sacrifices?

Intertwined with the attacks and counterattacks of the war in Europe, I have sprinkled many current events happening at the time back home in Canada — a country that you and Grandpa helped to settle. A young country, itself coming of age, Canada lost many of its young, productive people to the war overseas.

Jim has the last word. In a postscript to his final letter home from the hospital two days before his death, Jim reveals the type of son he was, Grandma: "Now Mother Dear, don't worry much about me as I will get alright."

1

THREE CHEERS — WE'RE AT WAR!

The date was June 28, 1914, when the gunshot reverberated all over Europe and England. Archduke Franz Ferdinand, heir to the Austro-Hungarian throne, was assassinated in Sarajevo, Bosnia, his beautiful young wife, Sophie, killed. For the month following that fatal shot, word flew around Europe — telegrams, communiqués, debate in the parliaments of all the major countries. The fine print in alliances made years before were read and re-read. Archduke Franz Ferdinand was dead. Nationalism had been surging all over Europe and Great Britain. An excuse for war, at last! War was imminent.

A throng gathered in Trafalgar Square in London, England, on August 4. As the clock in the tower of Westminster struck midnight, war was declared. A cheer went up. Street parties broke out. In Canada, crowds gathered in main streets, cheering, parading up and down, and singing patriotic songs. German soldiers leaving their homeland leaned out of train windows, shouting "On to Paris!" Equally confident, French soldiers and those of the British Expeditionary Forces rallied their troops with "On to Berlin!" All sides were certain the war would be over by Christmas.

— — —

Until the Statute of Westminster was passed in 1931, an Act of the Parliament of Great Britain was binding on the dominions. Consequently, the act declaring war on

Jim's attestation papers. Although Jim listed his birthdate as December 18, 1897, his "assumed age" was entered as 18 years and 7 months.

Germany meant that Canada and the other Commonwealth nations were obliged to support Britain. From Canada's prairies to its seashores, from the mines of Wales, to the sheep farms of Australia and New Zealand, from Africa, from India, from the halls of Westminster, and from across many continents, men and women answered the call to arms.

In Canada, a new country of little more than 7.8 million people, men joined up. Many boys lied about their age so as not to miss the "show" that would end in six months.

On July 21, 1915, in a small town in southwest Manitoba, three boys boarded the train to Winnipeg. For the occasion, they had changed from their everyday clothes into suits, ties, and hats. By the next day they would be proud members of the 79th Cameron Highlanders of Canada. The regiment, Winnipeg and Western Canada's first Highland regiment, was only five years old, having being established on February 1, 1910.

On August 5, 1914, when Ottawa enlisted a division for overseas service, the Cameron Highlanders in Winnipeg were only 497 men strong. Such was the loyalty and enthusiasm of Canadians that after a parade through Winnipeg on August 6, 1914, over one thousand men volunteered for the Camerons.

2

WHY ARE YOU GOING?

"Why are you going?" his mother asked from the step as she closed the farmhouse door behind her.

"Why are you going?" she asked as they drove to the burgundy train station slung low against the prairie sky.

"Why are you going?" she pleaded as she hugged him on the bottom step of the train, the last step before the whistle blew and he disappeared into the smoke and steam, and the sound of the grinding wheels gaining speed. Her question echoed over and over in the sound of the departing train — fading until it was gone. "Why are you going?" she whispered into the void left by the echo, into the silence. His mother's whispered words were on the tongues of mothers around the world.

As he closed the front gate behind him, Jim hadn't looked back at the home he was leaving. He hadn't answered his mother's question; not because he didn't want to, but because he couldn't. Nor did he ever give her an answer to that question — a question that reverberated with the constancy of shell fire as he crouched in cold, muddy trenches in a foreign land, far from the prairies he knew — the same unanswered question that haunted his dreams, his wakeful nights.

Why are you going? In his boy's mind there was no satisfactory answer then, not one that would have lessened the worry on his mother's face as the tall, sparse figure turned from the train growing silent in the distance — a frame once erect and now lessened by the unanswered question, the uncertainty of the future. Why was he

Jim and his family on the front porch of their home near Belmont, Manitoba, circa July 1915. (Left–right) Jim Fargey, Mrs. J. Fargey (mother), Aileen (sister), Mr. Sam Fargey (father), Frank (brother), and brother Cecil (front).

choosing to leave the three-storey brick home his parents had just finished building? Why was he leaving his bedroom looking out on the pond where the ducks took their young in spring, where he skated in winter? Why was he leaving his bed with the warm, crazy quilt a neighbour had made as a housewarming gift?

Jim had just turned 17. Like boys all over the continent, he followed his heart. Was it a heart filled with love of God and Country? Was it restlessness, a desire to see new places, to experience new things? Opportunistic young men grabbed at the

The boys board the train for Winnipeg, July 21, 1915. Though just 17, Jim was determined to join the war effort.

chance to change their futures — futures that, here at home, were often predictable, configured, and mapped out for them like a prairie road, with the beginning and end visible before the journey even began. Many dreamt of a bend in that road, a hill, a change in the landscape of their futures.

How long would she wait for his answer? She would wait, knowing the same sun warmed her son in the trenches. Each night she would trim the lamp wick, clean last night's soot from the glass chimney. By lamplight she would write the letters he would carry with him into the trenches, into nights occupied with mending the barbed-wire maze of no man's land. She would write letters that he would read and re-read. She would write; and she would wait for his return. Then an answer would be no longer necessary.

3

YOU'RE IN THE ARMY NOW!

Jim and his two friends, Leslie and Arthur, travelled a local line, not the Canadian Pacific, east to Winnipeg that morning in July of 1915. However, it was the Canadian Pacific Railway that was still causing excitement all across Canada — that amazing ribbon of steel which had threaded its way both east and west from Central Canada in only five years. When the Last Spike was driven on November 7, 1885, at Craigellachie, British Columbia, the CPR became the thumb that held the ribbon taut for the bow that tied the country together from sea to sea.

The CPR had been given a gift of 25 million acres (equal to about 100,000 square kilometres) of free land by the government for building the railway. The *Dominion Lands Act* of 1872 enabled the government to offer 160 acres of free land in the fertile West to any homesteader brash enough to take it and strong enough to work it.

Immigrants could also purchase a package that included passage on a Canadian Pacific (CP) ship, travel on a CP train, and land from the CPR for as little as $2.50 an acre, then ride across Canada inexpensively on railway cars equipped with sleeping facilities and small kitchens. In providing these amenities, CP created an economy for their railway and helped to settle a vast country. And immigrants did come! Canada's population grew from approximately five million in 1900 to just under eight million by 1914.

Within its first 30 years, this very same railway had brought Jim's father and uncles, and later his mother and many others, from Ontario to break the land and

Rank *Pte* Name PARGEY, James Henderson ✓ Reg'l No. 155395 P 59

Unit 79th C.H. of O. to If in perm. Corps, What Unit? Married or Single Single.
43rd Bn.

Place and Date of Enlistment Winnipeg, 22nd July, 1915. Place of Birth Belmont, Manitoba

Name and Address, Next-of-Kin Samuel Pargey,

Belmont, Manitoba. Relationship Father.

Assigned Pay Monthly $ 15 — Payable to *Mrs J Pargey, Belmont, Man* Relationship

Separation Allowance $ Payable to

Relationship

Discharge, Date and Place *Died of Wounds 15/10/16* Reason Character

Date		PAY			Field Allowance			Other Credits	Total Credits	Voucher		Cash Payments	Assigned pay	Other Charges	Total Debits	Balance	Remarks, Casualties, etc.
From	To	No. of Days	Rate	Amount	No. of Days	Rate	Amount			No.	Date						
Nov 1/30		30	1.00	30	30	.10	3	2760	6060			1704	30		4704	1356	15.00 a P for Oct Cr from Oct
Dec 1/31	1916	31	"	31	31	"	310		3410			2676	15		4176	570	
Jan 1/31		31	"	31	31	"	310		3410			973	15		2413	1839	
Feb 1/29		29	"	29	29	"	290		3190			1965	15		3465	1252	
Mar 1/31		31	"	31	31	"	310		3410			524	15		2024	2638	
				152			1520	2760	19480			84290			168412		

Checked *WHK*

BALANCE TRANSFERRED TO NEW LEDGER.

(above and right) **Records of pay and assigned pay. Jim was paid one dollar a day for his service. Of this, he signed over half to his mother: "I drew my $30, which was pay in full. I signed over $15 a month to Mother. We had to sign it over or the government would keep it for me and dear knows if I ever would see it again. It will go into effect as soon as I leave for the Old Country. $30 is too much to carry around."**

build homes in Manitoba — at the time just a small province that had been created on May 12, 1870, surrounding the Red River Colony. Its pioneers had hopes and uncertainties not unlike those of the three young men heading to Winnipeg to join the war effort during that summer of 1915. They all carried with them an excitement and a fear of what lay ahead.

MILITIA AND DEFENCE
ASSIGNED PAY
OVERSEAS CONTINGENTS

M. F. W. 12a.

Sheet No. 2. Mrs. J. Fargey

PAYMENTS. Name of Soldier *Fargey J. H.*
153395

L. L. Job

Month.	Year.	Cheque No.	Amt. $15.00	Remarks.
April	1916	R 613	15	
May		S 3615	15	
June		T 6885	15	Casualties
July		J 9990	15	
Aug.		P 13444	15	
Sept.		W 17333	15	
Oct.		W 22460	15	
Nov.				
Dec.				Account closed Nov
Jan.	1917			Acct closed Nov 1/16
Feb.				
March				T. X. Rend. Date ... By ...
April				E.F.X. " Date ... By ...
May				

Winnipeg, September 19, 1915

Dear Father,
I suppose you're threshing now. I see by the papers that pigs are a pretty good price. You'll be selling ours, I guess. We got our underwear the other day. It is certainly good stuff but a little heavy.

I drew my $30 which was pay in full. I signed over $15 a month to Mother. We had to sign it over or the government would keep it for me and dear knows if I ever would see it again. It will go into effect as soon as I leave for the Old Country. $30 is too much to carry around.

Your loving son,
Jim

Montreal, October 18, 1915

Dear Mother,
We arrived tonight. They marched us onto the boats and gave us berths. I
am sending you a picture of the boat. Everything is the same but where it
is painted white, it is black in times of war.

The British often considered the troops arriving from Canada an ill-disciplined, ill-equipped bunch, and sent them to the south of England to "shape up" for the realities of war.

In his memoir, *Riding into War*, Canadian veteran James Robert Johnston talks about his arrival at Shorncliffe, England, in the fall of 1916:

We started in training again in a day or two under Imperial
instructors. I still don't think the English instructors liked Canadians,
or they would not have drilled us so hard. It was right on the double
all day, bayonet practice, rifle practice, in and out of trenches, bomb
throwing and more running. I thought we were in pretty good shape,
but they soon showed us the difference. They kept this up for over a week
and I think they wanted to make it so hard for us that we would want
to go to France, or somewhere else.

In a letter to his older brother, Frank, Jim gives details of his daily life in England:

East Sandling, Kent, England, Nov 26/15

Dear Frank,
We are taking Musketry training now. Learning all about the rifle and
how to use it. After musketry we go to the ranges to practice shooting. Most

of us have the Lee Enfield rifles. They are lighter and shorter than the Ross rifle and are far better for shooting. The lads here never used a Ross.

IN THE TRENCHES

The Ross vs. the Enfield

Sam Hughes, Canada's minister of militia at the outbreak of the First World War, made several questionable decisions: one was to equip Canadian soldiers with the Canadian-made Ross rifle instead of the British Lee Enfield. Although his favourite was good for target shooting, it was ineffective in trench warfare, where it was prone to jam with mud and dirt. As well, the bayonet, when attached, tended to fall off when the weapon was fired. Soldiers in the field referred to it as "the old Sam Hughes." The Ross did, however, have a higher rate of fire, and snipers liked it for its long range and accuracy. Because of its deficiencies in the field, but over strong objections from Hughes, Prime Minister Borden authorized soldiers to replace "the old Sam Hughes" with the Lee Enfield rifle. Some 1,453 Canadian soldiers disposed of the Ross, and by the Battle of the Somme, the new commander-in-chief of the British Expeditionary Force, Sir Douglas Haig, had all three Canadian divisions armed with Lee Enfields.

Jim's letter continues:

> *I have just been home a week from my leave. We certainly had a fine time in Leeds. The kilts are the dress for getting "the Janes" to look at you on the street. They weren't very cold with a pair of underpants on but the worst trouble is that you have to wash your knees too often!*
>
> *I am on fatigue to-morrow. I can't kick as it is only the second fatigue since I came here. They say three Zeppelins flew over camp the other night*

but we did not see them. We have to cover up our windows every night at dark with blankets and the whole camp is in pitch darkness. We have gone out on two route marches this week already. We generally go out about seven o'clock and come in at nine. We do night work such as judging distances in the dark and judging sounds.

This morning we had scouting. It was rather interesting but hard work with your overcoat on, rifle and pack on our back. We have to carry our pack on our back every morning parade except an hour in the morning.

We get up at six-thirty. First parade at 15 to 7 for an hour. Come off parade at eight and go on again at eight forty-five. We have forty-five minutes at dinner and go on again till five o'clock. We are going all day and have to look after our rifle and clean our boots after supper.

Well, Frank, it is nearly bedtime. This is all I have to write this time.

Your loving brother
J.H.

When Jim later writes his younger sister and brother from the battlefields of Belgium, his opinion of the kilt has changed from his earlier letter to Frank:

April 11/16

Dear Aileen and Cecil,
Well, sister and brother, how are you getting along? You have written quite a few letters to me and I'm taking this opportunity of writing. We came out of the trenches the morning before last and are in the supports at present. George Money came over from England and landed here a few days ago but hasn't been in the trenches yet. They have the kilts and look fine but they are no use for the trenches, especially in the wet weather!

Jim, sporting the regimental kilt: "The kilts are the dress for getting 'the Janes' to look at you on the street. They weren't very cold with a pair of underpants on but the worst trouble is that you have to wash your knees too often!"

But Jim's opinion of the Ross rifle hasn't changed:

May 2, 1916

We are going into the trench with the Ross rifle. I thought before that we would have the Lee Enfield as we did our target shooting with it.

May 27/16

Dear Brother,
I am glad to hear that you are nearly finished sowing your wheat. The 49th battalion are in the trenches now. They generally camp around where we are. All the Canadians are near one another. We have had a draft from the 44th battalion to reinforce us. Quite a few fellows have got Lee Enfield rifles. They watch around and pick up old ones and clean them up. I have still got the "old Sam Hugh's" yet.

— — —

Each soldier's kit could mean the difference between life and death, and so he had to maintain it through mud, freezing temperatures, and blistering heat. At roll call each day the soldier had to produce his full kit.

After the artillery bombarded the enemy's defences, soldiers went "over the top." As they climbed out of the trenches and advanced toward enemy lines, most British and Canadian soldiers carried with them approximately 60 pounds of equipment: a rifle with fixed bayonet, 170–230 rounds of small-arms ammunition, grenades, a steel helmet, and later a gas mask, a pair of goggles against tear gas, a first-aid field dressing, and iodine. They also carried everyday living requirements: a waterproof groundsheet

IN THE TRENCHES

Iron Rations

Food supply was a major problem when soldiers advanced into enemy territory. All men carried emergency food called "iron rations." These iron rations could only be opened with the permission of an officer.

The kit contained an emergency ration of preserved meat, cheese, biscuit, tea, sugar, and salt. It was carried by all British soldiers in the field for use in the event of their being cut off from regular food supplies.

A typical iron ration for British soldiers in 1914 contained:

1 pound preserved meat
3 ounces cheese
12 ounces biscuit
5/8 ounces tea
2 ounces sugar
1/2 ounce salt
1 ounce meat extract

and cape, a filled water bottle, a haversack with a mess tin, personal belongings, one preserved ration, and one iron ration. Many carried shovels, and some had picks strapped to their backs. A small trench spade could save a soldier from being stuck in open land as well as provide him with a club for close fighting.

Soldiers stumbled across muddy land cratered by the bombing, unaware that artillery bombardments had rarely knocked out all enemy gun emplacements and barbed-wire fences. Armed with only a rifle and bayonet, and laden with heavy equipment, they were an easy target for the highly mobile machine gunners.

France, March 23, 1916

Thank you very much for the parcel. Those cotton rags come in very handy to use to clean our rifles, as cloths like that are very scarce and we have other bandages if needed otherwise. Those socks were fine but I have nearly enough socks now for a while and it is kind of hard carrying them around when we only have a small pack and have to carry everything with us.

IN THE TRENCHES

Hughes's Folly #2

Another Hughes "folly" had been equipping Canadian soldiers with MacAdam shield-shovels — he had ordered 25,000 of them. Although similar to the standard portable infantry spade, it was also intended to shield the soldier from bullets and allow him to sight the enemy through a large hole in the centre. This design, however, required heavier steel, which meant that each one weighed more than five pounds — making it understandably unpopular with men already carrying a 60-pound kit. It proved incapable of stopping gunfire penetration, and soldiers couldn't shovel soil effectively because of the sight hole.

4

REALITY

Feb 21, 1916, Bramshott, England
Dear Mother and Father,
We are leaving for France today. God bless you and keep you safe.

Your loving son, Jim
P.S. You talk about putting one's head up over the parapet. I have been
warned several times by fellows from the front. I will keep mine down.

Jim does not write what he was thinking as he marched up the ramp to board the ship, leaving relative safety of England for the unknown across the channel. Did he think of the mine blasts he heard frequently from France and Belgium while training in Bramshott? Was he remembering the bayonet practice in which he thrust a bayonet into a dummy stuffed with straw? Did he wonder if he would have the courage to do the same with a human body, to withdraw a bayonet dripping with another's blood?

His diary, too, captured actions, not thoughts or feelings:

February 21, 1916
Left rest camp and took boat over to Le Havre. Went to camp in Le Havre
and then to train in the evening. "Box Cars!"

Jim with backpack and gun, date unknown.

HOLD THE OXO!

LEST WE FORGET

Bramshott

Bramshott Military Camp was located near the village of Bramshott Common in Hampshire, England, southwest of London. The St. Mary's Church here holds the graves of more than 300 Canadian soldiers who had been stationed at the camp during the First World War. Ninety-five other Canadians who died in Bramshott during the First World War were Roman Catholics, and they were buried in Grayshott, four kilometres to the north, in St. Joseph's churchyard. Many of the dead were victims of the influenza outbreak of 1918. In fact, more people died of influenza between June 1918 and December 1920 than during the war — an estimated 50 million people — making it one of the deadliest natural disasters in human history.

February 23, 1916
On the night arrived at siding and walked to Eke. Left Eke Mar 1 and walked to Donought — twelve miles distance.

March 8, 1916
Left Donought for front lines "Messines" No. 2 platoon in reserve.

March 9, 1916
Left trenches and stayed in barn all night. Left in morning.

March 28, 1916
Left B camp for trenches in "Ypres salient" No. 2 platoon in reserve on Bydand Avenue.

Jim went into the battlefields of Europe as part of the 43rd Battalion in the 3rd Canadian Division and 9th Infantry Brigade of the Canadian Expeditionary Force (CEF). He was one of more than 600,000 Canadian men and women who enlisted in the CEF during the First World War as soldiers, nurses, and chaplains.

5

YPRES SALIENT

In the spring of 1914, Ypres, Belgium, was a beautiful and quiet medieval town. The famous Cloth Hall, the centre of the textile industry, stood bordering the market square as it had for 700 years. Flax fields reflected the blue of a cloudless summer sky. Ypres stood like a ballet dancer listening to the prelude of spring surrounded by a tutu of fields. Vegetables pushed their way through the soil and children went to school, skipped stones on the canals, and gathered eggs from the neighbouring henhouses. Birds sang from wooded ridges south and east of town, boats plied the river and canals winding north to the English Channel.

A counterpoint to children's skipping rhymes was a rumbling, like thunder, coming from the east — Germany was flexing its muscles. Its neighbours watched. Riveting noises from German shipyards signalled a buildup of its navy, a challenge to Great Britain's claim as monarch of the seas. People still hoped that, like faint and distant thunder, the slowly edging storm cloud of war would pass. Alliances and pacts were in place to prevent an outbreak of conflict. But alongside the vows of friendship and protection, a restless pride pulsed in the veins of both the European nations and Great Britain.

After that shot of July 28, 1914, the country of Belgium declared itself neutral. Unfortunately, the town of Ypres lay between Germany and the English Channel. Belgium was the access point for the shipping lanes and sea ports that would protect U-boat activity in Germany's "race to the sea."

Postcard showing the Halles of Ypres (Cloth Hall) in 1912.

The Halles of Ypres after the bombardment of November 22, 1914.

ON THE BATTLEFIELD

The Second Battle of Ypres

The early military uses of chemicals were as tear-inducing irritants rather than fatal or disabling poison. These gases had been used by both sides in the early days of the war.

Poison (chlorine) gas was used for the first time on the Western Front during the Second Battle of Ypres as the German 4th Army attacked French positions around the northern Belgian town. British and Canadian forces moved in and plugged the gap but were unable to regain any ground taken by the Germans. The British had withdrawn to a second line of defence, leaving Ypres still in Allied hands but virtually surrounded. Casualties in the Second Battle of Ypres totalled approximately 58,000 Allies and 38,000 Germans.

When Jim arrived at Messines, Belgium, in March 1916, the British Expeditionary Forces (BEF) were battling on the Western Front around Ypres. By then, the bravery of the soldiers fighting in the area was already legendary. They had defended the town during the First and Second Battles of Ypres (1914 and 1915) with only scant supplies and against overwhelming odds. The location of Ypres, in the only corner of Belgium not under German occupation, made the town a symbol of defiance.

But Ypres was no longer the pastoral town it was before the war. Booths in the square still sold Flemish lace hankies, postcards, and soap to soldiers, but it was a ghost town. A gas attack on April 22, 1915, accompanied by the shelling of Ypres, sent people underground, into drainage pipes and basements, where the roofs often fell in on them. The townspeople left for France as the bombardment continued. The spires and roof of the Cloth Hall and of St. Martin's Cathedral smouldered. Ypres was a city on fire; it was in ruins, but still undefeated.

6

IN THE TRENCHES

France, March 9/16
(Messines, south of Ypres, Belgium)

My Dear Mother,
Well, Mother, how is the weather in Manitoba? We had snow here two or three days ago but it is nearly all gone by now and it makes things rather sloppy although nearly everybody gets long rubber boots in the trenches and so keeps his feet dry. We are in the Reserve Trenches now and are billeted in farms back of the firing line.

Mac Woods is in a different company than I'm in but he is trying to get transferred so we can get together again. Things are very dear here with hardly any canned goods or anything and we do not get very much pay. I borrowed a pound from Mac as he happened to have some in the bank in London; so if you'll ask Father if he will take $5 out of my account and put it to Mac's credit. Mac said not to mind it but I don't want to owe him anything and be sure and take it out of my account as you said you were banking the money you got from the government. Now this doesn't mean to send me any as I have a pound now and I think it will be enough when I'm drawing my regular pay. We draw 1 franc a day now, that is about twenty cents and the remainder is *credited to us in England. There really isn't very much news to tell.*

With love to all from your loving son, Jim

In a letter home in August, Jim writes that

Mac is back with us again. I don't know how his feet will stand the marching as they are not in good shape, but mine are fine and I can stand the marching. It is the long marches and hard cobblestone roads that are worst but we don't have many long marches.

Did they know? Could anyone have known what they were trading the comforts of home for, whether a frame prairie homestead, a miner's cottage, or the solid brick house in the city? Could they imagine that their home away from home on the Western Front would consist of holes dug in the chalk and marshes of France and Belgium? Could they have guessed that they would share these stench-filled trenches with rats and lice and thousands of other soldiers — more people than lived in the town of Ypres? Could they have foreseen that their only protection from the North Sea seeping continuously up under their feet would be roughly thrown together "duckboards" underfoot and the rubber boots they were issued — that their view, if they dared lift their heads above the parapet, would be of shell craters filled with mud and decomposing bodies caught in the uncut mesh of barbed wire? And that the mere lifting of their head could invite the sniper's bullet? Could they have imagined the boredom of waiting cramped in the trenches day after day, uncertain of what might happen?

In the trenches at night, soldiers could sometimes hear their enemy's laughter and singing. From their respective trenches, day and night, both enemy and Allied "sappers" and "kickers" picked away at the earth under no man's land.

"No man's land," the narrow stretch of land between the enemy trenches, was

IN THE TRENCHES

Sappers and Kickers

In the chalk, "sappers" lay flat on their backs, barefoot, with sandbags lining the floor to silence the noise, and picked with bayonets fitted especially for the job. They softened the chalk with vinegar when necessary, caught the freed pieces in their other hand, and stored them in sandbags to be carried back to waiting cars on tracks. If they were lucky, they advanced about 18 inches in 24 hours; it was tedious work.

"Clay-kickers" had been used to tunnel under the streets of London to lay sewer, road, and railway works. The clay near Ypres resembled that of London, so the Mining Corp was formed. Clay-kickers used steel spades on their feet to dig out clay while lying on a wood cross. They could tunnel at the rate of about 10 feet per day. As the Germans also were digging tunnels, both sides developed listening devices to locate the enemy's tunnels. By 1918, the Mining Corps consisted of 60,000 members who were digging tunnels. They could then plant explosives under enemy lines — the enemy's position given away by the sound of their voices in the night, talking or singing songs of home.

where, on Christmas Day, 1914, a white flag was waved and the enemy soldiers shared handshakes, cigarettes, and stories of home. Later, though, generals discouraged such activities because opposing soldiers might develop friendships and lose their desire to fight one another.

— — —

By the end of 1914, trenches stretched for 765 kilometres, from the Swiss border to the Channel Coast. In some places, enemy trenches were less than 27 metres apart.

IN THE TRENCHES

Trench Foot

Much of the land on the Western Front was only a half-metre above sea level. As soon as soldiers began to dig trenches, the water would seep up from just below the surface. Constantly standing in water caused trench foot and other ailments. With trench foot, the feet would gradually go numb and the skin would turn red or blue. If untreated, trench foot could turn gangrenous and result in amputation. By the end of 1914, about 20,000 cases of casualties resulting from trench foot were reported by the British Army. Something had to be done. In an attempt to keep the soldiers' feet dry, wooden planking, known as duckboards, was placed at the bottom of trenches and across other areas of muddy or waterlogged ground to act as a dry bridge for the soldiers to cross. Waterproof footwear, extra socks, and regular foot inspections also helped to reduce the number of cases.

The front lines were manned by millions of men — infantry battalions, cavalry squadrons, artillery battalions, and pioneer companies. Backing these up were catering wagons, signal corps, pay corps, field ambulances, nurses, doctors, horses and their handlers, technical battalions, blacksmiths, carpenters, mechanics, meteorological units, aircraft units, veterinary units, map detachments, engineers, and many others.

The main trench and the communication trench were built in a zigzag pattern and broken by traverses to prevent crossfire and movement of shrapnel along the line. Since most of the land was only a few feet above sea level, the cold water seeped in as soon as soldiers began to dig.

Trenches, April 25/16

My Dearest Mother,

I rec'd your letter today dated Apr 2 and one also from the Bible class and it certainly is a fine day, the sun shining bright. It wasn't very good weather a few days ago but it has stopped raining now and the trenches were certainly in some mess while the wet weather continued but most of us have long rubber boots and do not notice the water so bad.

Mac and I are what they call wirers, that is fixing wires up in front of the trenches and having to work by night time and sleep in the daytime and we have to do our own cooking. You would be surprised to hear of what good dishes we have sometimes. The average dugout in the front line holds about two and you have to curl up in some peculiar shapes in some of them. There are three of us in the one dugout now and one lad had some rolled oats and we made porridge. It was the first porridge I've had since I left England and it was certainly good. We get the raw rations and ham to cook them ourselves. The greatest shortage we have is bread and all the troops in France seem to be short of the same thing. The food is good though and nothing to kick at.

Here I am sitting outside the dugout writing and the sun beating down, getting ready to move back to the reserves this afternoon.

I wish to thank you very much for that Easter card you sent. It certainly is a nice one. How did you spend your Easter Sunday? We were right in the front line Easter Sunday and didn't have any eggs either. If I had of been out in the billets I would have had a few as we usually live on eggs while in billets.

I hear there was a riot in Winnipeg between the soldiers and the policemen. They don't want to start to fight there as they can get all the fighting they want to do over in this country.

Do you receive all my letters because I write one every week and I like to know if you get them. Do you get my three pound regular every month? There will be quite a few pound saved up in England in my account when I get back as we only draw a franc a day here out of fifteen dollars a month.

You asked me how the sox were for size — well that pair that Aileen sent is just the right size and good and long in the leg and they are not too thick and easy to wash but I have plenty of sox already. Will you send a little tin of cocoa as it is very good in the trenches when you come in rather chilly. You needn't send any more Oxo. We don't use it much.

Well, Mother, this is about all the news I have this time.

With love to all
From your loving son
Jim

The first barbed wire used in the First World War was installed on wooden fence posts. This cumbersome work required three men to accomplish — one carrying the posts, another carrying the barbed wire, and the third hammering posts in place for stringing the wire. The noise of the pounding alerted the enemy snipers of the soldiers' presence and invited enemy fire — making it extremely dangerous work. With the development of "pigtails" (an iron corkscrew which could be inserted into the muddy no man's land), the task became easier and quieter, though still remained dangerous. At first, soldiers who needed to cross over the barbed wire had one soldier lie down on top of it as a human bridge. When all had crossed on top of him, fellow soldiers would lift him straight up carefully so as not to tear his skin. This practice was stopped when sharp porcupine-type spiked balls were laid under the fence by the enemy.

— — —

O.1285

Soldiers hunker down in dugouts or "funk holes" in the trenches. Date unknown.

A preserved tunnel at Vimy. In the 1920s the French government put aside a whole section of the ridge as a memorial park, preserving the trenches, shell holes, and mine craters.

What remains of officers' quarters in the trenches at Vimy.

As Jim sat outside the dugout writing, he could almost smell the bursting of leaves on the elms Father had planted around their new home for protection against the north and west winds. He could feel the rush on his face of moist warm air heavy with the smell of animals as he opened the barn door at milking time. The sun outside the trenches was warmer than it would be at home — more like a fall sun in Manitoba, when the wheat sheaves stood leaning against each other in stooks to keep out the rain. He thought of the smell of burning — of clearing land — of decaying leaves preparing for winter. It was a smell he enjoyed.

Instinctively, he covered his nose to block out the stench of the decaying corpses of men and horses in no man's land, of the stagnant water in the trenches, of thousands of his fellow soldiers, all in need of a bath and huddled in the trenches, where they repaired sandbags or wrote letters or played cards. Then there was the smell of fear, as the men waited for the next attack.

Down the line another soldier heard the crashing of the waves against the rocks near Peggy's Cove — the crashing noise that had frightened him as a boy now seemed like a distant murmur compared to the noise of the artillery barrages overhead, of shells pounding no man's land — creating a cratered landscape where two years before there had been freshly planted fields. He thought of being out on the boat with his father, hauling in the catch — of the smell of fish fresh from the sea, of kelp and salt, and the comfort of the mist on his face.

On the other side of Jim sat a man with his face to the sun. He was listening, waiting for the hoot of the owl, the howl of the wolf, or the cry of the loon. He saw wide open spaces as his parents had known them — a land where they could ride freely, wind in their hair. He felt the excitement of changing campsites in summer, of following his father on the trapline in winter. And he remembered fences — a creeping barrage across the prairie. Fences he had joined the army to escape. He looked out from his trench and saw the barbed wire fence and lowered his head.

7

SURPRISE WEAPONS

BARBED WIRE

It's the best fence in the world.
As light as air.
Stonger than whisky. Cheaper than dust.
All in steel and several miles long.
The cattle haven't been born can get through it.
Gentlemen, take up the challenge and bring your cows.
— John Warne Gates, barbed-wire merchant, Texas, 1870s

It was 1874. On a farm in Illinois a farmer was concerned about his recent loss of cattle. He wanted to protect his herd by keeping his cattle in and marauding wild animals out. He would like to let them graze in distant pastures without concern. He sat in the long evenings twisting wire and then twisting small, sharp pieces of wire onto a longer length of wire. His excitement in his invention lessened when the small barbs loosened and slipped down the wire. He tried again. He pricked his forefinger with a barb and stopped for a moment to suck out the possible infection. Finally, he took a second length of wire and twisted it around the first, keeping the sharp barbs in place.

J.F. Glidden had invented what would become an icon of the Midwest landscape and of the Canadian prairies as it undulated across the land, held taut by the upright fence posts. The prairie fence withstood the winds of summer and cast long shadows across the snow-white fields of winter. It would be the subject matter of art and song. As he worked the wire — forming and reforming — until it served his purpose, he could not have dreamed of the uses barbed wire would be put to just 40 years later. In those still, starlit evenings, the excitement of settling the West filled his thoughts, not the noise of bombardments where artillery fire smashed against the wire, deafening soldiers and blasting craters in the verdant fields of Belgium and France.

He could not have imagined that the wire developed to protect his cattle from harm would be used to catch and hang up human beings in its barbs, to hang them up as human targets for the gunfire of the enemy and sometimes that of their own comrades. When the searing prairie winds caught the tumbleweed and blew it against his fence, clasping it there through winter and summer, he would have been hard-pressed to see in its form the figure of a soldier soon to be caught just as firmly in the barbs on another continent. Barbs, sometimes a finger thick, were meant to maim — wires, not strung in an orderly manner, but criss-crossing one another, sometimes in coiled masses 40 feet wide, turning back on itself like a maze that seemed to have no beginning or end — a maze from which there was no escape. Wire strung across a no man's land as far as the eye could see, which had to be repaired after nightfall, and was often found uncut when the soldiers went "over the top."

J.F. Glidden would have shuddered at the thought of his invention becoming a symbol of a war that would last four years and claim the lives of approximately 19 million people and wound many more.

Wire-cutters in no man's land had one of the most dangerous jobs.

GAS

"Piss on your handkerchief. Piss on your undershirt. Piss on any rag you can find!" The command echoed up and down the Canadian lines. The most available rag was often the one the soldier used to clean his gun. A Canadian medical doctor, who was also a chemist, recognizing the smell of chlorine and knowing that uric acid would crystallize the chlorine, advised this to the infantry.

On the morning of April 22, 1915, Ypres was lit by the rising sun, its spires throwing shadows across the quiet square. The country surrounding the town rose slightly on the edges like an upside-down Frisbee, the 40- to 60-metre rise giving the Germans both a visual advantage and a direct line for artillery fire into the enemy's trenches. Reconnaissance reports of activity in German trenches seeped through, so the Allied forces were watchful. Coupled with rumours from a German deserter that his countrymen intended to release a special weapon, these reports raised the level of tension in the trenches.

The 1st Canadian Division, recently arrived from England, received orders on April 22, 1915, to move into the trenches northeast of Ypres. The fighting around Ypres during 1914 had created a bulge (or salient) in the British line that protruded into German-held territory. French colonial forces defended the north arm of this bulge, Canadians the northeast portion, and Britons the east and south. Because of this bulge, the German forces could cut off the Allied front if they were to gain access on either side.

Though the soldiers had seen the realities of trench warfare, they were unprepared for what greeted them in the Ypres Salient. Here the trenches were not only poorly constructed, with inadequate parapets for protection, but they had no traverses, or bends in their construction, to prevent being directly fired upon from the German trenches. The soldiers were also ill-prepared for the sight of decomposing bodies left lying in the surrounding battlefields and trenches.

The French trenches, built in the shape of half moons, were not connected to one another. Canadian troops, when they arrived, worked desperately against time to make the trenches safer. First they dug deeper and sandbagged them, then they spread barbed wire in front and prepared Gravenstafel Ridge, which lay behind the present line, as a secondary position in case they needed to fall back. The 2nd Brigade commander, Arthur Currie, decided it would be important to have a fallback position on the highest ground possible. This was known as Locality C.

By late afternoon the shadows had shifted east of the town, but they were invisible to the soldiers as flames leapt up against the setting sun. A gentle breeze fanned the fire's intensity. All day the German bombardment of Ypres had shattered houses and further damaged the Cloth Hall in the Market Square and the Cathedral of St. Martin behind it.

At precisely 5:00 p.m., the German soldiers opened up the valves on bottles of deadly chlorine gas. It flowed quickly through the lead pipes they had laid over the breastworks of the front-line fire trench. Within ten minutes, the hissing cylinders were empty.

IN THE TRENCHES

Poison Gas

The development in the use of poison gases led to both phosgene and mustard gas being used. Phosgene was especially potent as its impact was frequently felt only 48 hours after it had been inhaled, and by then it had already bedded itself in the respiratory organs of the body and little could be done to eradicate it. Also, it was much less apparent that someone had inhaled phosgene, as it did not cause as much violent coughing. By the time that phosgene had got into a person's bodily system, it was too late.

Mustard gas was first used by the Germans against the Russians at Riga in September 1917. This gas caused both internal and external blisters on the victim within hours of being exposed to it. Such damage to the lungs and other internal organs was very painful and occasionally fatal. Many who did survive were blinded by the gas.

Toward the French colonial lines, luminous yellow/green clouds carried a stench different from the putrid trenches, different from the burning of bricks and mortar. The clouds crept stealthily, carried forward by a light breeze. They rolled over the ground, and seemed to gather momentum as they advanced. Soldiers were blinded, their throats were burned; they coughed and vomited.

This new intruder was invincible — resistant to artillery fire and bayonets, impervious to barbed wire, ominous in its onslaught. At first the French forces fought on, but they finally had to turn and flee from this enemy they could neither identify nor combat. This left approximately 12 kilometres of the front line unprotected. Because of the salient, it would now be possible for the German forces to advance through this unprotected front, essentially cutting off the Canadians.

An hour later, the Canadian infantry were commanded to move into the flank vacated by the French forces — having little idea what lay ahead.

At the same time, the Germans were moving south, short of reserves and unaware that their way was open right into Ypres. At midnight, the 10th and 16th Battalions attacked the German positions in Kitchener's Woods, near St. Julien, and held the position.

The introduction to *The Selected Papers of Sir Arthur Currie: Diaries, Letters, and Report to the Ministry, 1917–1933* states:

> *Confusion reigned in the Canadian and British lines.... Currie appears to have acted calmly and coolly under pressure. He deployed his battalions to tactically important ground and managed to hold off the German advance. Two days later, the Germans unleashed a second cloud of gas, this time against the Canadians. The German assault came close to breaking the Canadian line, opening up gaps between the 2nd and 3rd Brigade. Currie requested British reinforcements, but received inconclusive responses. After instructing the commander of the 8th Battalion, Lieutenant Colonel Louis Lipsett, to withdraw if he deemed it*

Wikimedia Commons.

The Canadian St. Julien Memorial, located at Vancouver Corner, Ypres Salient, Belgium. Also known as "The Brooding Soldier," it commemorates the sacrifice of the Canadian 1st Division, in action April 22–24, 1915, at the Second Battle of Ypres. Some 2,000 Canadians were killed, wounded, or reported missing in action during the battle.

necessary, Currie went back to the lines of General Headquarters to personally find and muster the reinforcements needed to plug the gaps. Although these were the actions of an unconventional commander (he probably should never have left his headquarters), they demonstrated that Currie trusted his subordinate commanders and was willing to take the personal action to protect the men under his command. The next day the German attacks were renewed but the Canadians again held their ground, and the British and French forces were able to counter-attack or reinforce the wavering line that the Canadians had held against all odds.

In his gas course notebook, Jim writes:

August 13, 1916

Care of Helmet
a) Helmets will stand two gas attacks
b) See that helmet is properly folded
c) Regularly Inspected — once every week, daily during gas alert
d) Replaced immediately after gas attack if worn in gas, also after they have been rolled up on chest for twenty-eight days and nights and after they have been worn in shell gases twenty four hours
e) Never dry helmet if wet or breathe into it unnecessarily because this destroys the chemicals
f) Eye pieces should be treated once a week with "Glasso"

Throughout April, the Germans launched a "hate shoot" against Ypres, leaving it in shambles, but undefeated. Saving Ypres from German occupation became a rallying point for the Allied forces.

WORDS OF WAR

Dulce et Decorum est

Bent double, like old beggars under sacks,
Knock-kneed, coughing like hags, we cursed through sludge,
Till on the haunting flares we turned our backs
And towards our distant rest began to trudge.
Men marched asleep. Many had lost their boots
But limped on, blood-shod. All went lame; all blind;
Drunk with fatigue; deaf even to the hoots
Of tired, outstripped Five-Nines that dropped behind.

Gas! GAS! Quick, boys! — An ecstasy of fumbling,
Fitting the clumsy helmets just in time;
But someone still was yelling out and stumbling
And flound'ring like a man in fire or lime…
Dim, through the misty panes and thick green light,
As under a green sea, I saw him drowning.

In all my dreams, before my helpless sight,
He plunges at me, guttering, choking, drowning.

If in some smothering dreams you too could pace
Behind the wagon that we flung him in,
And watch the white eyes writhing in his face,
His hanging face, like a devil's sick of sin;

> If you could hear, at every jolt, the blood
> Come gargling from the froth-corrupted lungs,
> Obscene as cancer, bitter as the cud
> Of vile, incurable sores on innocent tongues, —
> My friend, you would not tell with such high zest
> To children ardent for some desperate glory,
> The old lie: Dulce et decorum est
> Pro patria mori. *
>
> — Wilfred Owen (1893–1918)
>
> *The last two lines translate from the Latin as "It is sweet and honourable to die for one's country."

AIRPLANES

Although trenches were a new development, tanks a new invention, and gas a surprise, possibly the greatest advancement in technological warfare in the First World War was in the air.

Only 11 years after the Wright Brothers made their first successfully controlled flight, visionaries realized that the airplane would become an integral part of war, while others still saw its use as for reconnaissance only.

At the beginning of the war, hot air balloons (eyes in the sky) equipped with a powered winch that could bring them down quickly, if necessary, provided a means of spying on the enemy. Messages dropped from these balloons or from light aircraft informed the artillery below of enemy movements so the artillery could make

"The Best Noose of the War," by cartoonist Captain Bruce Bairnsfather, a young Scotsman who fought at the front during the First World War.

corrections to the firing battery. But balloons were very vulnerable to artillery fire. Carrier pigeons were also used to transport information over long distances.

In order to save weight, the earliest flights of the war carried only a pilot. By September 1914, developments in wireless transmission allowed observers to identify the enemy's position and approaching planes and then to inform the artillery. Radio transmitters, however, weighed 75 pounds and occupied one of the two available seats in a plane; thus, each pilot had the stress of having to navigate, fly, observe, and transmit results, all at the same time.

The Royal Flying Corps (RFC) was, for the first time, able to take aerial photographs. The camera was usually fixed to the side of the aircraft or operated through a floor-mounted aperture.

The Royal Flying Corps (RFC) was made up of men of courage, men who knew that their chance of survival was slim if their flimsy planes went down — parachutes were not provided at the time. By the end of the war, the Wright Brothers may have been hard-pressed to recognize their invention of 1903.

Until machine guns were mounted onto the planes, pilots carried a pistol, and sometimes a rifle, to shoot at enemy aircraft. Some were known to carry small grenades or bombs to drop over the side, onto the enemy below. One of the more daring RFC missions was to deliver spies behind enemy lines and supply them with carrier pigeons to transport messages back to base.

Machine-gun fire caused much damage to the wooden propellers of the aircraft, and this forced many pilots to crash-land their planes. A French pilot, Garros, solved this problem by adding wedges of steel to divert the bullets. It worked for a while, but when Garros's plane crashed and he was captured before he was able to burn the plane, the Germans recovered it intact and proceeded to copy his design, adding a synchronizing gear in which the propeller was linked by a shaft to the trigger to block fire whenever they were both in line. This gear allowed the firing of a forward-facing gun through the propeller without striking the wooden blades — this revolutionary aircraft was the Fokker. This technology gave the German air force a temporary advantage and dominance of the skies in 1915. Known as the "Fokker Scourge," this dominance would last nearly a year, until Allied aerial technology could catch up.

Even knowing the hazards of flying and the possibility of instant death, 23,000 young Canadian men (most under the age of 25) joined and went into combat after approximately 30 hours of flight training. Of these, 1,388 were killed — many before they ever saw action. Because of the high death rate, by 1918 most of the pilots were between the ages of 18 and 21. The Royal Flying Corps drew men from across the British Empire; eventually nearly one-third were Canadian.

On April 1, 1918, the Royal Flying Corps became the Royal Air Force (RAF).

TANKS

In his plans for the Battle on the Somme, July 1, 1916, General Douglas Haig pinned some of his hopes for success on the introduction of a new secret weapon being developed by the British — the tank. However, moving the date of the offensive ahead meant that they had not yet produced enough of the new vehicles.

A shipment of 49 tanks finally arrived in France in late August. They were introduced for the first time in a major battle that took place on September 15: the Battle of Flers-Courcelette. Lumbering like oxen at a mere 5.5 kilometres per hour across no man's land, crushing barbed wire fencing in their path, the "monsters" raised terror in the German ranks. Many of the enemy soldiers turned and fled. The tanks were most effective in clearing out German snipers in ruined villages. By the end of the first day of fighting, the heavily fortified villages of Flers, Martinpuich, and Courcelette had been captured.

In spite of the initial impact of the tanks, there were problems with them. Many became mired in the craters and uneven, muddy terrain of the battlefield, or suffered mechanical breakdowns. And many were hit and badly damaged by German artillery. In spite of these problems, with the help of the tank the Allies gained in seven days as much ground as they had between July 1 and September 14. This gain raised the morale of both generals and soldiers.

Spurred on by the success of September 15, tanks were again employed successfully in the September 26 capture of Thiepval Ridge (a German vantage point overlooking the British front line).

ON THE BATTLEFIELD

Tank Warfare

The first-ever appearance of tanks on a battlefield occurred during the Battle of the Somme as British troops attacked German positions along the five-mile front, advancing 2,000 yards with the tank support. The British-developed tanks, the Mark Is, featured two small side-cannons and four machine guns, and were operated by an eight-man crew. As the infantry advanced, individual tanks provided support by blasting and rolling over the German barbed wire, piercing the frontline defence, and then rolling along the length of the trench, raking the German soldiers with machine-gun fire. Initially called "land ships" by the British Army, they were referred to as "water-carriers" (later shortened to "tanks") to preserve secrecy.

Unlike in the Second World War, Germany had very few tanks active in the First World War, with only 15 (A7V type) being produced in Germany during the war.

By the end of the Battle of the Somme, in spite of their limitations, tanks had proven themselves as weapons with great potential for the future battles of the war.

8

A DAY IN THE LIFE

France, March 15/16

Dear Father,
At present we're billeted in a barn and have very comfortable quarters
and plenty of straw to lie on. They are fine billets and it is something
to be able to stretch out and have a good sleep. The average dugout in
the front line holds about two and you have to curl up in some peculiar
shapes in some of them.

"Stand-to" was a part of every soldier's life. Leaders believed that raids were most likely during early dawn or in the evening, when visibility was low. Thus, soldiers in the front trenches were wakened an hour before dawn to take their position on the fire step of the trenches, ready for an attack. They repeated this procedure in the evening. After morning stand-to, soldiers cleaned their guns before breakfast in preparation for a later inspection by their commanding officers. In some battalions, the cleaning of guns was enhanced by a shot of rum.

Life in the trenches involved a daily routine of filling sandbags, draining or repairing trenches, preparing latrines, and repairing duckboards. After the chores, daytime activity in the trenches was restricted because of snipers. This quiet time would be spent writing letters home, playing cards, catching up on lost sleep, and preparing meals.

Courtesy Canadian War Museum 19920085-137.

Mail Arriving at a Canadian Field Post Office.

Normally, soldiers spent three to six days in the front trenches and then were moved back to the support lines. Occasionally they would be allowed a short leave in

HOLD THE OXO!

a nearby French village. In the following letters written in the early spring of 1916, Jim adds further details about the everyday life of a soldier at the front:

March 2, 1916

Dear Frank,
At present we are only three or four miles from the firing line and can hear the big guns booming very plainly. We aren't going up for a few days as the battalion that we are going in with are out resting at present. Two of our company went in last night and I guess Mac Woods was with them.

It is very muddy here but the worst of it is over and the trenches are beginning to dry up. It is rather hard to write when you are sitting on the tent floor writing by candlelight.

We are going into the trench with the Ross rifle. I thought before that we would have the Lee Enfield as we did our target shooting with it.

When you get this letter you will be busy putting the crop in — pulling the lines over a four-horse team. Many's the time I wish I was back again but we are soldiering now and have to put up with a few things. It is the long marches and hard cobblestone roads that are worst but we don't have many long marches.

Eatables are very dear in France and about all you can get are eggs and chops. We only draw a franc a day now; that is about 20 cents.

Your loving brother Jim

March 5, 1916

My dear Mother and Father,

It snowed here yesterday and it makes things rather wet. We are in tents now and we are in very comfortable quarters. I have met several fellows who have been out here for a year and safe yet and believe me I'm going to keep my head down.

Well Mother and Father I have some news to tell you. You might not be pleased at first but I think you will consider it. I have started to smoke, not smoking steady but take a pipeful of tobacco occasionally. It gets so lonesome sometimes in the tent that it helps to pass the time away and one needs something to keep your nerves steady especially in a heavy bombardment. I don't smoke very much but I considered it before I started and I thought that you wouldn't mind it considering the circumstances.

With love to all.

Another chum from Winnipeg and I read our Bible chapter by candlelight every night possible.

From you loving son
Jim

April 8, 1916

My Dear Mother,
Last letter you asked me if I needed any drawers or shirts. Well I'm wearing drawers at present and the weather is beginning to get warm so I don't really need any in a short time. We have a bath and change of underwear about every two weeks and I really couldn't carry any more in my pack as it is heavy enough now. I have plenty of sox but I guess those two pairs are on the road by now but there are some lads here who are short so I'll give them a pair or so. I don't need any kneecaps as we do not wear the kilt.

HOLD THE OXO!

Did you get that 3 pound I sent from Bramshott? You don't want to bank it but keep it for yourself as spring is coming on and you'll need it for flower seeds and etc.

The order just came in that we're going for a bath tomorrow. That certainly is joyful news as I need one and a change of underwear.

With love to all
From your loving son Jim

On Good Friday (April 21, 1916), Jim wrote in his diary, "Left E camp for the trenches." The next month he wrote:

May 15, 1916

Left B camp and went to the trenches. Trench 59 Bay 12. Spent four days in front line and moved to supports in Cumberland Dugouts. Got shelled every day for four days. Sgt. Maj. Morrison killed.

Lice, which the soldiers called "grey-backs," troubled the men in the trenches. Often the lice lived on in the seams even after uniforms were steamed and cleaned. After leaving the front line, soldiers would bathe in large tubs with many other soldiers to get rid of the smell of the trenches. Before their bath they left their clothes to be cleaned. After bathing, they collected their clean uniforms. The men were checked for lice, as they could carry dangerous diseases.

May 3/16

Dear Frank,
Rec'd your letter yesterday and was glad to hear from you. I wish I had

been home to help you break in those colts as I generally used to like that job. I suppose you will be breaking the sorrel pacer some of these days and then you won't be able to see the buggy for dust.

About all the animals we see around here is "grey backs" (which resembled grains of uncooked rice) and we have a picnic every time we come out of the trenches picking them off our shirt but if we hadn't anything worse than these to bother us we would be Jake. If you would ask Mother to send a little bagful of sulphur to put around my neck as they say that will kill them although I'm not bothered very much with them.

We all heard about that big riot in Winnipeg between the soldiers and police and most of the fellows said to send them out here and they would get all the fighting they want and they can send our battalion back and will keep peace alright.

From your loving brother
Jim

May 8/16

My Dear Mother,
At present we are back at a rest camp for a few days and we certainly enjoy getting where we can buy things and where we can stretch our limbs. It is a treat to get in a Y.M.C.A where we can write letters and there is a singsong every Sunday night and a band concert thro the week. Yesterday they held church parade and it was a treat for the whole battalion to meet once again and hold service. You were mentioning in your letter about the paper mentioning about the Canadians being in the thick of the fight but our battalion and a number of others were not in the thick of it at all.

The newspapers often hear funny rumours.

There has only been one communion since we have been in France and unfortunately I was on duty all that day. Dr. Gordon was away for a while when we came over first but he came the second time we went into the trenches with us and has been with us ever since. We will have service tomorrow in the Y.M.C.A and that will be our last Sunday out before we go back to the trenches.

There certainly will be plenty of water in the ground and in the sloughs there this spring. I guess Cecil will have quite a time with his raft on the slough. I am glad to hear that the hens are laying well. Eggs are quite a price here — two for 9 cents in your money but we can afford them now and again as we save money for a few days while in the trenches.

Today was supposed to be our big sports day but I guess it is called off on account of the rain. We have been playing football and baseball and are having a fine time since we came out. It relieves the monotony of things and there is a band concert every night in the Y.M.C.A.

With lots of love to all
From your loving son
Jim

May 27/16

Dear Brother,
The 43rd baseball team played the P.P.C.L.I. and beat them about 8–2. We have certainly some baseball team. Most of them are Regina fellows. We have had a draft from the 44th battalion to reinforce us. Quite a few fellows have got Lee Enfield rifles. They watch around and pick up old

"S'pose we'll 'ave to stop behind and tidy all this up when it's over, Bert."

"A Tidy Job." Sketch by Captain Bruce Bairnsfather. Humour helped to keep the soldiers' morale up during their time in the dangerous and uncomfortable trenches.

HOLD THE OXO!

ones and clean them up. I have still got the "Old Sam Hugh's" yet, that is what the lads call them.

Your brother,
Jim

Sometimes a mere 640 metres from the front, soldiers printed a newspaper called *The Wipers Times* ("Wipers" being a play on the British pronunciation of *Ypres*). Richard Westwood-Brookes from Dominic Winter Book Auctions, who recently sold

---

WORDS OF WAR

Extra! Extra!

The Wipers Times *was a trench magazine produced by some English soldiers who were stationed on the front lines at Ypres, Belgium. In early 1916 they had come across an abandoned printing press and decided to start printing material for and by the soldiers. Though originally called* The Wipers Times *(for the slang name the English had for the town of Ypres), the name of the publication changed as the troops advanced, at one point being called* The Somme Times. *There were even two editions published after the war ended entitled* The Better Times.

These magazines encouraged participation by the troops, who would submit their poems, advertise fake plays they were producing, and write advice columns. These were light-hearted in order to relieve the stress of the soldiers' lives in the trenches. One advice column suggested: "Now, when on patrol work and you hear the words 'Ach Gott! Ich bin gauz fed-up gerworden' issue from an unknown trench, this does not necessarily signify that you have worked too far over to your left and stumbled into the French lines!"

---

what was thought to be the very first *Wipers Times* published, said: "*The Wipers Times* was intended to be a … good laugh before they were all blown to bits. It is an incredible monument to them. The fighting was at its fiercest when they were producing it." The editor was Lieutenant Richardson, and its sub-editor and publisher was Captain F.J. Roberts. The paper reportedly was printed on an old press found in a hedge.

In spite of the light-heartedness, the reality and sound of war was never far off. In his diary, June 2, 1916, Jim writes, "Stand to all day and moved up to Tillebeck dugouts in the evening. Big battle in the loop of the salient. CMRs [Canadian Mounted Rifles] and PPCLI [Princess Patricia's Canadian Light Infantry] cut up. Fritz explodes a mine and takes trenches, also Sanctuary Wood. Heavy casualties."

The Battle of Mount Sorrel was underway, with the Germans eventually capturing key Allied positions — Mount Sorrel, and Hills 61 and 62 — north of the Ypres-Menin Road.

On June 3, 1916, Jim writes, "Moved into the Communication trench between Maple Copse and Sanctuary Wood as a front line."

On June 4 the 43rd Cameron Highlanders cleared Maple Copse, occupied Border Lane, and successfully repulsed a counterattack. Jim chronicled his movements over the next week in his diary:

> *June 5, 1916*
> *Moved into trench in Maple Copse in strong point. Bombardment very heavy. Several killed.*
>
> *June 7th*
> *Got relieved by the 52nd Batt and went to the Belgian Chateau.*
>
> *June 9th*
> *Left Belgian Chateau and went up to the trenches. No. 2 platoon went to S.P.*

June 11th
Left S.P. and marched to the Belgian Chateau.

June 13th
Left Belgian Chateau on a forced march to Tillebeke dugouts and stayed
there till the next evening. Rained for the last couple of days and trenches
in bad mess.13th and 16th Batt. took back trenches lost on June 2nd and
took quite a few prisoners. Quite a few casualities.

Writing home on June 17, Jim reassures his mother and father, "I guess you've been anxious about me. We have been having quite a time these last two weeks but I came through it safe. Don't worry. I am in fine health and a good rest will fix us all up fine."

While Jim was writing this letter home to his family, 20,000 sappers were tunnelling under the Messines Ridge. A year later, on June 7, 1917, as the Third Battle of Ypres (Passchendaele) began, the 19 mines planted by these sappers were detonated, blowing the Germans off the Messines Ridge to the south of Ypres. The blast was heard from as far away as London. In the three years since the war began, this would be the first significant movement in this section of the line.

Throughout the summer of 1916, Jim's letters home described manning the trenches in this area. By August 27, 1916, his diary records that they were marching and travelling by train toward the Somme. They arrived in Aberle, where they were billeted until September 6. During that time, Jim records that drill is the order of one day, a gas course another.

9

BATTLE OF THE SOMME

Why the Somme?

For nearly a century, military historians have debated why the Somme was chosen as the launching site for a joint French-British attack and for the first major British offensive of the war.

The Somme, a quiet river weaving its way across the undulating countryside of northeast France to the English Channel, was not a major front in the ongoing war. The Germans were entrenched already with deep bunkers, using the slopes of the surrounding hills for protection.

General Haig would have preferred more time to prepare. However, the French were experiencing heavy fighting near Verdun and General Joffre felt a unified offensive would divert some of the German strength northward. General Haig finally agreed that when the grounds dried in the spring they would launch a unified offensive along the 70-kilometre front. This would involve well over one million troops and was meant to overwhelm the enemy.

The Somme battlefield itself was small (stretching approximately 24 kilometres with a depth of up to nine kilometres) but it claimed 300,000 British, Commonwealth, French, and German soldiers' lives between July 1 and November 19, 1916; twice as many soldiers were wounded.

Generals Haig and Joffre finally agreed on July 1, 1916, as the date and the Somme as the location for the initial attack.

Horses and men hauling in supplies through ankle-deep water and mud, April 1917.

Preparations began in earnest. Imagine the commands being given, the scurrying to carry out orders. Imagine the secrecy and need for stealth. Imagine the chaos, the anticipation. Imagine the apprehension, night and day.

HOLD THE OXO!

Trenches that the British had taken over from the French at the end of 1915 needed reinforcement of their parapets, parados, and fire-bays, and barbed wire needed to be installed in no man's land. The sound of marching boots on cobblestones and the staccato of horses' hooves drifted over the surrounding countryside as 400,000 men and 100,000 horses were moved to the Somme.

"Moles" quietly implanted dynamite under no man's land. Carpenters, blacksmiths, mechanics, aircraft units, doctors, nurses, ambulances, catering wagons, signal corps, and map detachments prepared for the fight under a closer deadline than earlier anticipated. Three hundred trucks of drinking water were hauled in. One very important aspect of planning was to establish a clearing station where the seriously wounded could be brought for treatment before being transported by train to a hospital near the coast.

ON THE BATTLEFIELD

Trench Runners

A runner was a soldier who was responsible for passing on messages between fronts during the war. This was arguably one of the most dangerous jobs, since these soldiers had to leave the safety of the trenches or bunkers in order to move from one front to the other. While on the open ground, the soldier was completely exposed to enemy lookouts, and it was common for runners to be killed, often by snipers, before they had reached their destination. This is why most runners worked under cover of darkness. Many were highly specialized — efficient at reading maps and at reconnaissance — and they generally worked in pairs. Adolf Hitler was a runner for the German army during the First World War, and he was wounded twice. Runners were often decorated for bravery, and Hitler was no exception, receiving both a second-class and first-class Iron Cross during the war.

By the time the Second World War broke out, radio and telephone communication had replaced runners completely.

Communications were one key to success. The Allies installed 11,000 kilometres of buried telephone wires plus 70,000 kilometres of above-ground cables. The military would need phones, telegraphs, runners, dogs and pigeons, flares, flags, and horns to alert all those along the front and in the air what was happening. A long blast would ask "Where are you?" The answer would come through a pre-arranged variety of coloured flares. The life expectancy of a "runner" during battle was measured in hours.

— — —

Although the Australians' method of attack at Pozieres during the Battle of the Somme was for the men to fan out and circle behind the German lines, the British still favoured the frontal attack, where soldiers advanced shoulder to shoulder. This foolhardy plan used by the British at the Somme had been tried previously by the French — it had failed.

The British generals were confident even though the great losses suffered by the French fighting desperately near Verdun meant they would not be able to support the British at the Somme.

Engineers built railways across 89 kilometres of chalky countryside with 17 railheads — two of which would be used as ambulances to carry away the wounded. Soldiers moved into the front lines, backup trenches, and communication trenches. Excitement and optimism mixed with fear surged up and down the lines. For six days beginning on June 24, the Artillery bombarded the enemy with 1.5 million shells, hoping to damage trenches, cut barbed wire, and demoralize troops by cutting off the food and water supply.

On the evening of June 30, a special order was read to all the soldiers. Among other instructions, it warned: "The use of the word *retire* is absolutely forbidden, and if heard can only be a ruse of the enemy and must be ignored."

When the six-day bombardment and constant noise ended, silence descended

John McCrae's dressing station, which is located beside the Essex Farm Cemetery, several kilometres from Ypres, Belgium.

over no man's land. Alerted by the silence (which suggested an imminent attack), the Germans emerged from their deep dugouts, where they had been safe during the barrage, and manned their guns in readiness for the onslaught.

In the early morning of July 1, Allied trenches facing the enemy across no man's land were crowded and teemed like anthills. Like ants, each soldier moved silently but purposefully.

The British command to "fix bayonets," followed by "over the top," travelled along the entire 22.5-kilometre front. Side by side, soldiers climbed out of the trenches and raced across a no man's land of skeletal trees, cavernous craters, and a maze of barbed wire, most of which had remained intact despite the bombardment. As the soldiers moved forward into the tangle of wire, the German bullets found their mark. Before the day ended, it was apparent that the attack had failed: 19,240 British soldiers had been killed and approximately 38,000 were wounded (the British army's greatest loss in one day in history). Casualties dangled from uncut barbed wire or lay helpless and wounded on the field. After attending church on July 2, General Haig visited two Casualty Clearing Stations and noted later in his diary that the high figure of casualties and deaths "cannot be considered severe in view of the numbers engaged, and the length of the front attacked."

By mid-October the British battalions had become so decimated that it was difficult to muster 400 men for an attack. It was apparent that the Battle of the Somme would be won by the side that had the most men to sacrifice.

— — —

Immediately behind the trench system were the "dressing stations,' which were operated by the Field Ambulances. There were no facilities to perform surgery here, but men had their wounds dressed before they were sent back to one of the Casualty Clearing Stations (CCSs).

A typical dressing station had been set up in the basilica at Albert: "Wounded flooded in on foot, or were brought by stretchers, wheelbarrows, carts — anything. Their wounds were dressed and then they were laid out on the floor to await evacuation. Soon the whole church was packed and we were ordered to stop any vehicle that passed and make them take wounded to the rear. I even put three cases in a general's staff car. Those who were not expected to survive were put on one side and left. It was very hard to ignore their cries for help but we had to concentrate on those who might live. We worked for three days and nights without rest. It was the bloodiest battle I ever saw." (Private H. Streets, 58th Field Ambulance, from *The First Day on the Somme: 1 July 1916*, by Martin Middlebrook.)

In a memorandum to the War Committee in London on August 1, 1916, British member of Parliament Winston Churchill commented, "We have not conquered in a month's fighting as much ground as we were expecting to gain in the first two hours." In 1940, Churchill became both prime minister and minister of defence.

On that first day of battle, Newfoundland (at that time Britain's smallest dominion) was the only dominion force fighting on the Somme. The Newfoundland Regiment, held in support near the village of Beaumont-Hamel, had its instructions and was ready to go. After the failure within 30 minutes of the first attack by the British, the communication trenches became clogged with bodies, and flares were not being sent up as planned. Widespread miscommunication resulted in an order for the Newfoundland Regiment to attack. Now the Germans could concentrate their full artillery on the advancing Newfoundlanders. Approximately 800 brave men from the regiment attacked — only 68 answered roll call the next morning. In villages throughout Newfoundland, most of their young men would never return home. The Canadians would not join the Battle of the Somme until late August/early September.

In mid-August, troops confronted another enemy almost as threatening as the one that lay in wait across no man's land. The skies opened up and pelted the land with rain, making great swamps of the grain fields. The Canadians arrived to a scene of ashen villages, limbless trees, and a no man's land dotted with crater graves filled with mud, water, and decaying corpses. The thick mud would cake on their trench coats and pull the rubber boots off their feet.

Earlier that summer, on June 8, Jim had written to his mother from the Ypres Salient: "So your hired man is anxious to get the kilts. If he was in the trenches a few times and it [was] raining he would not be quite so anxious, especially when the bottom of them get[s] clogged up with mud — but luckily we have had very good weather while in the trenches."

Later the same summer, Jim wrote to his father about life on the farm back home, with no mention of the conditions he was facing in the trenches:

France, Aug 25/16

Dear Father,
I think I owe you a letter as it is sometime since I wrote to you. Very sorry to hear that you had some of your crop hailed out, but I suppose there were some who got hailed out completely. I am glad the Inspector was around and you insured your crop.

So Cecil is helping with the crop this year. When I get back he will be able to drive a four horse team.

Any time you ever want any money, Father, you can draw it from that $15 that comes home every month for me.

From your loving son
Jimmie

On September 3, Jim wrote, "I have been taking a course at a gas school for the last few days. We are back of the firing line at present and drilling very steady; but we are away from the roar of the guns and it certainly is a pleasant change and it rests your nerves a little. Today is Sunday and in the early morning the church bells can be heard ringing in the distant towns. The French go to church in the early morning."

At the Somme, attack and counterattack had led to virtually no advancement during two months of fierce fighting. The objective (the four-kilometre long Regina Trench) lay only two kilometres away. This see-saw back and forth, with both sides in turn advancing and retreating, would continue through early September. Jim's diary chronicles the move of the Third Division from the Ypres Salient toward the Somme:

> *Sept 14/16*
> *Left the camp in the bush on top of hill 4:00 p.m. and arrived our next camp eight p.m. one mile from Albert. Bivouaced for the night.*

> *Sept 15*
> *Left camp and marched through Albert about one mile the other side. Bivouaced for the night.*

As he marched through Albert, did Jim look up at the Golden Virgin statue holding her child, now hanging precariously atop the basilica spire? Had he heard the superstition that the war would end only when the Madonna finally fell?

Only when the Germans advanced into Albert in the spring of 1918 did the British Artillery deliberately target the statue, toppling it into the rubble below, so that their enemy could not use the tower as an observation point.

On September 15, 1916, the German front line — the Sugar Refinery, Candy Trench, Moquet Farm (later recaptured by Germans), part of Courcelette, Fabek Graben — was taken. This one-and-a-half-kilometre advance provided guarded optimism. Tanks, the British "secret weapon," brought in under the noise of artillery fire and hidden from view, surprised the enemy. Of the six tanks assisting the Canadians, one failed to start and only one really helped in the offensive. Although many were hit by German shell fire or suffered mechanical difficulties, those able to advance penetrated more than 1.8 kilometres — the most successful advance since the battle had begun on July 1.

> *Sept 16th*
> *Saw about thirty prisoners coming down. Four officers among them.*

Left place 4:30 p.m. and walked towards the trenches. Spent the night in trench near the Chalkpit.

Sept 18th
Left Chalkpit and proceeded to the front line. Relieved the 60th. Rained all evening.

The 43rd Battalion entrenched near Courcelette, where they would attempt to clear the high ground overlooking the River Ancre. On September 20, D Company, 43rd Cameron Highlanders, captured part of the Zollern Graben, a large trench that ran from Thiepval to just west of Courcelette.

That day Jim writes in his diary: "Went from front line to Bombing post in 'No Man's Land.' D Company took Fritz front line but had to retire after holding for eight hours on account of shortage of ammunition. Nearly whole company wiped out."

September 20, 1916, was the last entry in Jim's diary. He did, however, continue to write letters home:

September 29, 1916

My dear Mother,
Some of the Canadian mail came in yesterday but I didn't receive a letter from you; but expect one today.

It has been raining all morning but hope it will stop soon. The last trip in the trenches was very wet and it makes it very unpleasant and I hope it clears up before we go in again.

Mac has been having quite a bit of trouble with his feet and they sent him down to the base. I am glad, as his feet are flat and he is unable to stand any heavy marching at all.

Well Mother, the French and British have been making good progress on the Somme front and have taken quite a few prisoners so it should shorten the war up and I hope it will soon be over.

With love to all
From your loving son
Jim

Regina Trench was the longest German trench on the Western Front — four kilometres long, it snaked along the Ancre River and was only two kilometres from the Canadian jump-off line by September 15. It was guarded by three trenches — the Fabeck Graben, the Zollern Graben, and the Hessian Trench — which had all been captured by the Allies by the end of September. The Regina Trench was now only 600 metres from the new Canadian front line, but would evade capture for another six weeks.

After three months of fighting, the advances in the latter half of September — small though they were — allowed the generals optimism as they planned for the next large offensive, which was planned for October 1.

France, Oct 1/16 Sunday

My dear Mother,
I received your long letter today and was very pleased to hear from you. We are having beautiful weather now, especially today, the sun is shining but the nights are very cool. While I was in Bramshott I sent a scarf to London to Leslie Smith's grandmother for [her] to keep for me as I had one when I came over and she is going to send it over as it gets rather cool in the evening.

Was sorry to hear that you had so little wheat, but if the price keeps up it won't seem to be so bad. I suppose flour is up in price and will likely be up all winter. We get good bread here and generally enough; but now and again there are short rations. The Germans use black bread and you should see some of the prisoners eat our white bread. They work on the roads around here and get so much a day. They seem to be well satisfied.

I enjoyed your letter today and thank you for the scripture chapter as I read my chapter every night when I possibly can.

We had service this morning and communion after the service. Major Gordon is certainly a good minister and is well liked among the boys.

From your loving son Jimmie.

ON THE BATTLEFIELD

The Toll of the Great War

Due to the scope of the damage inflicted during the First World War, despite intensive research by historians, there is no definitive list of the casualties suffered in those years. The following numbers are estimates only.

Canada: 66,573 soldiers killed; 138,166 wounded*
The Colony of Newfoundland: 1,593 soldiers killed; wounded unknown*
Great Britain: 703,000 soldiers killed; 1,663,000 wounded
France: 1,385,000 soldiers killed; 4,266,000 wounded
Belgium: 13,000 soldiers killed; 44,000 wounded
Italy: 460,000 soldiers killed; 947,000 wounded
Russia: 1,700,000 soldiers killed; 4,950,000 wounded
United States: 117,000 soldiers killed; 204,000 wounded
Australia: 59,000 soldiers killed; 152,000 wounded
New Zealand: 18,000 killed; 55,000 wounded
Romania: 200,000 killed; 120,000 wounded

HOLD THE OXO!

Those who had fought against the Allies suffered heavy casualties as well:

Germany: 1,718,000 soldiers killed; 4,234,000 wounded
Austria-Hungary: 1,200,000 soldiers killed; 3,620,000 wounded
Turkey: 336,000 soldiers killed; 400,000 wounded
Bulgaria: 101,000 soldiers killed; 153,000 wounded

Other nations that suffered losses include Greece, India, Japan, Montenegro, Portugal, Serbia, South Africa, as well as many other countries in Africa and the Caribbean. The total deaths of all nations who fought in the war is thought to have been close to 8.5 million, with 21 million being wounded.

* Royal Canadian Legion website
All other figures from The Longman Companion to the First World War *(Colin Nicholson: Longman, 2001), 248.*

That first day of October broke — a sunny day. Most of the Canadian efforts along their area of the Regina Trench failed except for taking of the Kenora Trench, which gave a connection to the Regina Trench. The 2nd and 3rd Canadian Divisions attacked. Before the attack took place, scouts had reported that the wire was very thick and that it appeared untouched by the artillery. Only one small gap existed on the left. In trying to find this gap, practically the entire company was wiped out. One officer and the remainder of the company did reach the Regina Trench and stayed in position until 2:00 a.m., when they fell back.

Bad weather delayed further attacks until October 8, when the rain finally cleared.

In the darkness just before 5:00 a.m. that day, rumours abounded that the bombardment had not severed the barbed wire as planned, that many of the shells were duds and still lay unexploded in no man's land.

That last few minutes before the "over the top" order was given, each man was alone with his thoughts as he tightened his pack, checked his gun, fastened on a bayonet — alone with the question *Will I have the courage?*

Was Jim alone? Or did the voices of family and friends — voices that for over a year he could only imagine behind the words written on paper — come to him before he stepped out onto that battlefield? Certainly, those letters he had carried into the trenches with him, which held those voices from home, sang into the dark so that he did not feel he was alone.

As night fell on October 8, held up by the uncut barbed wire and enemy machine-gun fire, the Canadian Scottish Battalion were pinned flat to the ground at one point, with their commander, Major Lynch, dying from his wounds. Piper

LEST WE FORGET

The Unknown Soldiers

Those individuals who reached a hospital in a safe area behind the fighting lines and who died of their wounds would usually be buried in a cemetery near to the hospital, often in an existing town or village cemetery or in a specially created burial plot. These burials could be registered and their locations marked.

But thousands of soldiers were buried on the battlefields in individual or communal graves by their comrades during the fighting. They were often buried where they fell in action or in a burial ground on or near the battlefield. A simple cross or marker may have been put up to mark the location and give brief details of the individuals who had died. Early in the war many of these burials were not formally recorded with the soldier's name and the location of the grave.

The difficult task for the graves registration services was made worse by the nature of the fighting on certain battlefronts, such as the Western Front, where siege and trench

warfare meant that fighting often moved back and forth over the same ground. Between battles, day-to-day survival in the trenches and the hazards of exploding artillery shells, snipers, and grenades resulted in many casualties from sickness and wounds.

Many were lost when underground tunnels collapsed as they were being dug in order to set explosives under enemy positions. Conditions in the landscape also added to the number of casualties. Heavy rain could turn the fields into a sea of mud. Accounts by soldiers during the 1917 Battle of Passchendaele at Ypres tell of men drowning and disappearing in the waterlogged shell craters and deep mud.

Graves and burial grounds near the battlefronts were often damaged by fighting across the same location, resulting in the loss of the original marked graves. Some bodies simply could not be retrieved.

Added to this, the technological advancement in the weaponry used by both sides often caused such horrible injuries that it was not possible to identify or even find a complete body for burial. These factors combined to create a high number of "missing" casualties and for the many thousands of graves for which the soldier's identity is described as "Unknown."

Jimmy Richardson asked, "Wull I gie them wund (wind)," and proceeded to walk back and forth in front of the uncut wire playing his bagpipes, ignoring the enemy shells falling all around him. Hearing the pipes and seeing the piper's courage, the soldiers jumped to their feet and stormed the Regina Trench; they held it for just a short while.

The Regina Trench became known as the "Ditch of Memory" — only six officers and 67 other ranks responded to roll call the following morning. It was in this battle that Jim was seriously wounded in the leg and thigh.

Did Jim crawl through mud or was he carried by stretcher-bearers from the field of battle? Perhaps he almost welcomed the stabbing pain from his wound just to be away from the din of constant artillery fire and the fear of being hit, or worse still, being a target for enemy fire on uncut wire? Did he fear the doctor's diagnosis when he saw the mutilated thigh and hip? Did his medical officer in the trench, on seeing the seriousness of his wounds, wave him through to the Advanced Dressing Station for further attention, from where he was sent farther back to the Casualty Clearing Station? We know that Jim was finally sent by train or ambulance convoy to Étaples, home to one of the larger hospitals serving the wounded. The hospital was bombed later in the war by the Germans, on May 19, 1918.

On the night of October 10, the Third Canadian Division began to be replaced by the newly arrived Fourth Division. The exhausted First, Second, and Third Canadian Divisions withdrew from the Somme, having lost 20,000 men and having gained less than one kilometre since September 23.

On October 12, an experimental "creeping barrage" (later perfected at the Battle of Vimy Ridge) was introduced. The men moved forward at a pace of 45 metres each minute just behind an advancing barrage of Allied artillery explosions. Since the creeping barrage was new and experimental, with little time for preparation, confusion was rampant. One in ten of the attackers were killed either because the soldiers moved too quickly or because the shells fell short of their targets.

The wet and cold weather — rather than a decisive victory for either side — finally ended the Battle of the Somme on November 19, 1916. On November 18, the Allies reached their objective of the second German trench line north of Courcelette and captured 620 prisoners. When the Battle of the Somme ended, the line along the River Ancre had not advanced beyond the British objective for the first day of fighting — three and a half months earlier. The Allies now did have Beaumont-Hamel, Beaucourt, and Saint-Pierre-Divion in their possession, but were still nearly five kilometres short of Bapaume, which they had hoped to capture in early July. In his book *The Battle of the Somme*, Martin Gilbert estimates that the combined losses at the Somme and Verdun was on average more than 6,600 men killed each day — that's 277 casualties every hour, an average of approximately five men every minute. Families across Canada mourned the death of approximately 8,000 Canadians.

Thiepval Memorial to the Missing is the largest of all the Western Front memorials. On it are remembered, by name, 73,335 Commonwealth and South African soldiers whose bodies lie unidentified in the battlefield mud.

10

WOMEN IN WAR — THE BLUEBIRDS

Many of the war's "nursing sisters" died at the front along with the foot soldiers or died at sea along with the seamen. They nursed wounded prisoners, tended gunners, bandaged generals, drove ambulances, and wrote letters home for wounded soldiers. On June 27, 1918, 14 nursing sisters gave their lives aboard the hospital ship *Landavery Castle* when it was torpedoed by a German U-boat. Before the armistice was signed, 46 of the nursing sisters had died in the line of duty.

But in the Canada of 1914, Canadian women were not considered "persons." Although Canada had become a nation half a century earlier, its women were non-persons; they were legally excluded from voting. Their grandmothers had had it better. Before Confederation, women could vote if they owned property, although few actually did. The passing into law of the *Dominion Elections Act of 1906,* however, decreed that "no woman, idiot, lunatic or criminal shall vote."

In spite of the fact that they could not elect their own government, Canada's nursing sisters answered when the call came for Canada to fight alongside Britain in the First World War. When Britain declared its support of France on August 14, 1914, Canada had five permanent force nurses and 57 reserves. By the end of four years of the war in which the most human lives in history were lost, 3,141 nursing sisters had served in the Royal Canadian Army Medical Corp, 2,504 of them overseas.

Because of their blue uniforms, the soldiers in the trenches fondly called them "Bluebirds." Soldiers had no doubt about the nursing sisters' "personhood" as they saw them moving among the wounded, who were being transported by stretcher from no man's land to the Casualty Clearing Station close to the front line. The Bluebirds applied tourniquets to severed legs, bandages to mangled faces, and comforted the soldiers until an ambulance could transport them to a nearby hospital. These women worked with rudimentary equipment among the rats and lice and fleas. Exposed wounds on un-bathed bodies and under filthy conditions made soldiers extremely vulnerable to infection. The Bluebirds did their very best under those extremely difficult circumstances.

In the 1917 Canadian federal election (sometimes called the "khaki election"), the Bluebirds were among the very first women to vote legally in a Canadian election. They met the requirement enabling military personnel to vote under the newly passed *Wartime Elections Act*.

Historian Michael Bliss described the 1917 election as the "most bitter election in Canadian history." It was fought over the issue of conscription. Sir Wilfred Laurier, head of the Liberal party, opposed conscription. To ensure victory for conscription, Prime Minister Sir Robert Borden introduced two laws to skew the voting — the *Wartime Elections Act* and the *Military Voters Act*. The first law deprived conscientious objectors and Canadian citizens born in enemy countries who had arrived after 1902 of the right to vote. This act also allowed mothers, wives, and sisters of servicemen to vote.

The second new law allowed soldiers serving abroad to choose the riding in which their vote would be counted. Government officials could guide the strongly pro-conscription soldiers into voting in ridings where they felt it would be most beneficial.

In 1918, all Canadian women were given the same voting privileges as men in federal elections.

WOUNDED

26 General Hospital
B.E.F. France
Ward 10
October 12, 1916

Dear Mrs. Fargey,
You will have heard that your son has been seriously wounded in the right
leg, and although his condition is serious at present; we hope to send him
to England as soon as he is fit to travel.
*   He is very good & brave & hopes this news will not worry you too*
much. He is getting every attention here & just now is not in very much
pain. Your son will be able to write himself soon & I will let you know
again how he is getting on.

Yours sincerely
A. Sadleir
Staff Nurse-in-Charge Ward 10

Jim himself writes to his mother on letterhead bearing the YMCA logo and
beginning with:

On Active Service
WITH THE BRITISH EXPEDITIONARY FORCE
France Oct 13/16

My Dear Mother,
Sister told me she has written and explained the nature of the wound.
Now Mother I expect you will have heard of me being wounded long ago
as they took my name and number at battalion dressing station but this
letter will satisfy you more.

I am under the best of treatment and there is no danger at all. It will
be some time before I get any of your mail but I will write regular myself.

It is nice to be lying in a bed again and being fed on the best of food.
I had porridge this morning, the first for months.

I hope that Lance Corporal hasn't confused you as I just got made one
a couple of days before I went up to the trenches.

Well, Mother, this is all for now.

With love to all
From your loving son Jim
P.S. Now Mother Dear don't worry much about me as I will get alright.

But just two days later, Staff Nurse Sadleir writes to Jim's mother with worrying news:

15 Oct 1916

Dear Mrs. Fargey,
You will be grieved to hear that your son has become much worse & now
his condition is very grave; he is very quiet and has no pain, but I feel I

must let you know that the doctors fear that the end is very near. He is having every attention & is still quite conscious.

Your brave son continually speaks of you and sends his love to all. He has just had his minister to see him and he seems quite happy & peaceful.

I shall write to you again later
With love from your boy
Believe me
Yours sincerely
A.M. Sadleir, Staff Nurse in Charge

A second letter, written later the same day, confirms the worst:

15th October 1916

Dear Mrs. Fargey,
Your grief will be great when you know that your son passed quietly away this morning. He was so good and brave and did not murmur once.

He was anxious that you would receive his Bible and just a few things he had with him. He sent his love to all & then peacefully gave himself up. He was one of the finest lads I have ever seen — & an absolute hero; & I am afraid your sorrow will be great as he spoke continually of you & hoped it would not worry you too much.

It may be a little comfort to you to know that everything that was possible was done for your boy, & know that all the soldiers' graves are well kept & I shall put flowers on your boy's cross with your love.

With sincere sympathy for you in your great loss.
Believe me

Yours sincerely,
Angela M. Sadleir

During the few days in which Jim was hospitalized before his death, Sister Angela Sadleir had hand-written three letters home to his parents apprising them of his condition. The following is a letter from Chaplain W. Pitcairn Craig, who had visited Jim in the hospital:

These Four Boys Left Belmont to Fight For King—One Dead, Two Wounded

Corpl. A. Abbiss, Pte. L. D. Smith, wounded; Pte. G. Morley, J. H. Fargey, who was wounded October 8, ... died ... his injuries.

"These Four Boys Left Belmont to Fight for King — One Dead, Two Wounded" read the headline in the *Belmont News*. Shown are Corporal Arthur Abbiss and Private Leslie D. Smith (both wounded), and Private G. Money. James Henderson Fargey, our "Jim," is seated. On the back of the picture is a handwritten note stating that Arthur Abbiss had also died in the war.

23rd General Hospital
A.P.O S. 11
B.E.F.
16.10.1916

Dear Mrs. Fargey,
I have no doubt that by this time you have heard the very sad news of the death of your son L/C Fargey, who passed away in Hospital 26 yesterday forenoon. I saw him for the first time on Friday, and shall long remember with pleasure and thankfulness my visit to him. He did not seem then to be very seriously ill, and he told me much about his home, and how you had brought him up in the love of Christ and of what was pure and good. He said that it was that that had kept him fine and strong to ... the many temptations of army life. Before I left he asked me to read him a passage from the scripture, and on my taking out my own Testament, he begged me to read it from the Bible his mother had given him which he said he had never failed to read day by day.

On Saturday I had to be away from here all day — and yesterday (Sunday) morning, I received a message that your boy wished to see me. I went immediately and found him evidently near his end. He was, however, quite conscious, and asked me if I would, when all was over, write to you and say that he died happy and that his last thoughts were with you. After prayer with him, I had to leave him as it was the hour of my morning service — and, by the time I got back, he had passed away.

May I express my deep and warm sympathy with you in the great sorrow that has come upon you — and my hope and prayer is that, amidst your grief, you may be comforted and cheered by the thought that your boy laid down his life a sacrifice in the noblest of causes, that he died in the

faith and peace of Christ, and that now he has gone to receive the reward
the awaits a good soldier of Jesus Christ.

I am, yours sincerely and sympathetically
W. Pitcairn Craig
Chaplain
In due time your son's personal effects will be delivered to you by the
authorities.

Mac Woods had worked in the bank in Belmont before enlisting at age 17. Jim and Mac became very close friends while they served in the same company. Unfortunately, Mac's flat feet caused him great pain during long marches so he was sometimes posted to office duty. After the war, Mac would return to Belmont, marry his sweetheart on New Year's Eve, and move to a farm nearby. He would later buy the general store and bakery in the next town, Ninette. On hearing of the death of his friend, Mac expresses his loss in a letter of sympathy to Mrs. Fargey:

153658 Traffic Control
c/o Major Phillips
Town Major A.P.O. (S.52)
B.E.F.
France, Nov. 14th, 1916

Dear Mrs. Fargey,
Oh Mrs. Fargey I received the terrible news today from mother of dear
Jimmie's death and don't know when ever in my life I felt so bad over
anything before, as Jimmie and I were like brothers and when I was in
the battalion we never were apart for where you saw one, you would see
the other, and I shall never forget what he has done for me for the things

are too numerous to mention but I feel I owe him a terrible debt which now I shall never have the pleasure to return.

I have had many of boy friends in Canada and also since I have joined the army but have not seen or ever met one that can compare with Jimmie, for we have never had a cross word and the least little thing he could help me or any of the boys, Jimmie was always first and with such a kind heart and cheerfulness. If ever there was a boy to be proud of it was Jimmie, for I will say there is not a man in the 43rd Battalion (and all the boys in A Company will say the same) that would beat him as a soldier. How better could one die knowing he has done his bit to save his King and country like Jimmie has done, Mrs. Fargey. None that I can think of and nobody else, I don't think can. It is an honour that shall never be forgotten and we have to thank God for such men as those who have given their lives for us.

If it is God's will, Mrs. Fargey, that I shall return to see you all again, I shall love to talk of the times Jimmie and I have spent together. I would love to have someone here to-night who knew him, so that I could talk of the many kind things he has done for me, as I miss him more than writing or words can ever tell.

God help and give you strength, Mrs. Fargey, to bear the loss of such a brave and noble son, who always thought of his mother and did exactly as he knew she wished him to do.

Please give my kind regards and strongest sympathy to Mr. Fargey, Aileen and the boys as well as yourself. Hoping this finds you all the best of health.

Always yours very sincerely
Mac

Charles W. Gordon was the well-known author Ralph Connor and the chaplain of Jim's Division. Jim had mentioned him often in his letters as the chaplain who visited the trenches every evening:

On Active Service
SOLDIERS' INSTITUTE
Chaplain Service, Canadian Corps
14. 11.1916

My dear Mrs. Fargey,
You have reason to be thankful to God for all he has done for you — for He has given you a wonderful courage and faith in a time when faith and courage are sorely needed. You say that I perhaps did not know your boy. But I did — and remember well his fine manly soldierly bearing. He was a splendid fellow and you do well to be proud of him. I wish I knew more of his death. But all we know is that he went forward with his company and did his duty — got this wound — a very bad wound in the leg — I fancy his thigh was broken — of this I am not sure. But you may be quite sure he received every care and comfort. It was a terrible day for the 43rd — our losses were proportionately very heavy — but we are proud to know that our boys went steadily forward — without faltering — reached the German wire — which was found uncut except in certain spots — some of the boys went through these lines into the trench and past the trench on to the second objective — but of these very few came back. As the General of the Division said to me afterwards "Had it been humanly possible the 43rd would have won their 'objectives' — It was an impossible proposition and our boys did all that men could do."

You may well be proud of your son — He died a hero, doing his duty in the midst of the most terrible storm of shell and machine gun fire.

Jim's burial plot at the cemetery at Étaples, France, 1916. Today the location is well-tended and marked with a granite stone.

HOLD THE OXO!

What more can you ask — He gave himself for our great cause — and in this sacrifice you share. God will not forget nor refuse to accept this offering your boy has made — nor the daily sacrifice you make in bearing so heroically your great sorrow.

With sincerest & respectful sympathy
Yours sincerely — Charles W. Gordon
Major — 43rd Bn
Sr. Chaplain 9th Can. Inf. B'de

When the 43rd battalion left the Somme, there were 257 men left out of the 1,000 who had arrived. The Battle of the Somme would not be the last battle name etched into the memories of Canadians. The next two years would add many others — among them Vimy and Passchendaele — each with its own special meaning in the history of Canada.

ELEVENTH MONTH,
ELEVENTH DAY,
ELEVENTH HOUR

Today, you can still hear the echoes of marching boots on cobblestone roads, of anguished sobs from the battlefields, of comrades' laughter floating over now pastoral fields of the Ypres Salient, and the rattle of the artillery barrage on the River Ancre or bullets whizzing overhead, ricocheting off the uncut wire in no man's land.

But the echoes reverberate most loudly from the names carved in stone on the Menin Gate, on the Thiepval hillside memorial, and from the memorials and headstones in tranquil cemeteries dotting the countryside where soldiers lie — some of their names are known, but many remain unknown. In his poem "Have You Seen My Boy Jack?" author and poet Rudyard Kipling, on the loss of his son at the Battle of Loos, echoes the grief of all those loved ones left behind:

"Have you news of my boy Jack?"
Not this tide.
"When d'you think that he'll come back?"
Not with this wind blowing, and this tide.

Crowds gather at the Menin Gate Wall of Remembrance for the Last Post ceremony, Ypres, Belgium.

Kipling and his wife found it hard to accept that their son had been killed and that his body had never been retrieved. The author's grief prompted him to join the Imperial War Graves Commission (now the Commonwealth War Graves Commission), the group responsible for the care of the Commonwealth war graves. It was his suggestion that the words "Their Name Liveth for Evermore" be added to the Stones of Remembrance in the war cemeteries.

HOLD THE OXO!

The Menin Gate, Ypres, Belgium.

For graves of the Unknown Soldier, like his son, he could not accept only the inscription A SOLDIER OF THE GREAT WAR, and suggested KNOWN UNTO GOD be added across the bottom of the stone.

Each night at precisely 8:00 p.m., all evening traffic stops under the Menin Gate in Ypres, Belgium. The echoes from the past form a background orchestra for the playing of "The Last Post." Words carved indelibly into our hearts and souls for nearly one hundred years join the echoes:

They shall grow not old, as we that are left grow old
Age shall not weary them, nor the years condemn
At the going down of the sun and in the morning
We will remember them.

— "For The Fallen," Laurence Binyon

We will remember!

Jim's bible containing an inscription by his mother: "Remember thy Creator in the days of thy youth. July 23, 1915." As he lay dying in hospital, Jim asked the Chaplain to read to him: "... on my taking out my own Testament, he begged me to read it from the Bible his mother had given him which he said he had never failed to read day by day."

HOLD THE OXO!

WORDS OF WAR

Vimy

This Canada,
eighty-five hectares
a gift of gratitude

Loam rich with decomposition of bone, marrow, blood, flesh, sinews, sweat.
Echoes of guns, screams, tramping boots fading with time
The sun of this Canada does not span a continent from sea to sea
Does not floodlight golden carpeted canola fields framed in mountain shadows
Does not reflect diamond waves breaking against shores
This sun warms poppied fields whose blood red blossoms
Tiptoe across silent graves.
Winds winging across our Canada, over oceans, over channels
Weep on this Canada
And make verdant Hill 145, disguising wounds, camouflaging scars, silencing
exploding shells.
This Canada a sanctuary
of silent prayers, of memories, of unrealized dreams
Rising heavenward in marble
A young woman forever
Looks down on purple hazed villages in valleys
Cows in pastures, young men sowing seeds
and mourns her nation's loss.

Old now
These who are ours lie buried
in this Canada
our blood red maple leaf clings listlessly
against the flag pole here, mute testimony to
fading memories wisping across this land — this Canada
A part but apart.

— Marion Brooker

Statue (Canada Bereft) looks down from the Canadian National Vimy Memorial.

TIMELINE

1914

June 28	Archduke Franz Ferdinand, heir to the Austro-Hungarian throne, is assassinated in Sarajevo, Bosnia.
August 1	Germany declares war on Russia.
August 3	Germany declares war on France.
August 4	Britain declares war on Germany after German troops invade neutral Belgium. The United States declares neutrality.
August 5	The governor general of Canada (Field Marshal His Royal Highness The Duke of Connaught) officially declares war on Germany.
August 20	German forces occupy Brussels, Belgium.
October–November	The First Battle of Ypres is fought; the onset of winter weather forced a break in hostilities.
December 24/25	British and German soldiers interrupt the war to celebrate Christmas, beginning the Christmas truce.

1915

January 19	Germany begins an aerial bombing campaign against Britain using Zeppelins.
March 10	The Canadian Expeditionary Force saw their first battle of the First World War in the French town of Neuve Chapelle. It was also the first time aircraft had been used effectively for aerial photography and strategic planning (and also for bombing).
April 22–May 25	The Second Battle of Ypres is fought.
May 3	John McCrae writes "In Flanders Fields."
May 7	The RMS *Lusitania* is sunk by a German U-boat off the coast of Ireland, killing an estimated 1,198 people.
May 31	The first aerial bombing of London occurs. German Zeppelins kill 28 people.
July 21	Young Jim Fargey boards a train for Winnipeg to join the war effort.
July 22	Jim's attestation papers are filed, and he becomes a member of the 79th Cameron Highlanders of Canada.
August 1	The "Fokker Scourge" begins over the Western Front as German pilots achieve air supremacy using the highly effective Fokker monoplane featuring a synchronized machine gun that fires bullets through the spinning propeller.
September 6	The first prototype tank is tested for the British army.
September 26	The French launch their third attempt to seize Vimy Ridge from the Germans in Artois. This time they secure the ridge.
October 12	British nurse Edith Cavell is executed by a German firing squad for helping Allied soldiers escape from Belgium.

| December 25 | British and German forces declare a Christmas truce, get out of the trenches, and have a kick-around football game in no man's land. |

1916

February 21	The Battle of Verdun begins in France.
July 1–November 18	More than 1 million soldiers die during the Battle of the Somme, including 60,000 casualties for the British Commonwealth on the first day.
September 15	The first appearance of tanks on a battlefield occurs as British troops attack German positions along a eight-kilometre front during the Battle of the Somme.
September 25	British and French troops capture several villages north of the Somme River, including Thiepval, where the British successfully use tanks again. However, heavy rain turns the entire battlefield to mud, preventing further advances.
October 8	Jim Fargey wounded in assault on Regina Trench.
October 15	Jim Fargey dies in hospital from his wounds suffered at the Battle of the Somme.
November 18	The Battle of the Somme ends with the first snowfall as the British and French decide to cease the offensive. The Germans have been pushed back just a few kilometres along the entire 24-kilometre front, but the major breakthrough the Allies had planned never occurred. Both sides each suffered over 600,000 casualties during the five-month battle. Among the injured German soldiers is Corporal Adolf Hitler, wounded in the leg by shrapnel.

1917

April 6	The United States declares war on Germany.
April 9–April 12	Canadian troops win the Battle of Vimy Ridge.
June 5	Conscription begins in the United States.
June 13	The first major German bombing raid on London leaves 162 dead and 432 injured.
July 24	The *Military Service Act* is passed in the Canadian House of Commons, thanks to the support of nearly all English-speaking members of Parliament, and in spite of the opposition of nearly all French-speaking MPs.
July 31	The Third Battle of Ypres, also known as the Battle of Passchendaele, begins when Allied offensive operations commence in Flanders.
August 29	The *Military Service Act*, allowing conscription, officially becomes law in Canada.
November 6	After three months of fierce fighting, Canadian forces take Passchendaele in Belgium.

1918

January 28	John McCrae dies of pneumonia at Boulogne, France.
March 3	Germany, Austria, and Bolshevist Russia sign the Treaty of Brest-Litovsk, ending Russia's involvement in the war.
March 21	The Second Battle of the Somme begins.
March 30–April 1	Conscription Crisis of 1917: On Easter weekend, a man is arrested in Quebec City for not having his conscription registration papers on him. The incident sparks a weekend of rioting as the crowds loot the offices of the army registrar and smash the windows of English shops. Four civilians are killed and dozens injured.

August 8	Battle of Amiens: Canadian and Australian troops begin a string of almost continuous victories with a push through the German front lines.
November 11	Germany signs an armistice agreement with the Allies between 5:12 a.m. and 5:20 a.m. in Marshal Foch's railroad car in Compiègne Forest in France. It becomes official on the 11th hour of the 11th day of the 11th month.

1919

June 28	The Treaty of Versailles is signed in the Hall of Mirrors at the Versailles Palace near Paris, France. The treaty is signed by the Allied nations and by the defeated Germany. In it, Germany takes full responsibility for starting the war, loses more than 12.5 percent of its land area, and is ordered to pay millions of dollars in reparations to Allied nations — the final payments were not made until October 4, 2010, 92 years after the end of the First World War.

1936

July 26	King Edward VIII unveils the Canadian National Vimy Memorial, designed by Walter Seymour Allward of Toronto, Canada. The memorial had taken 11 years to construct.

2007

April 9	After undergoing extensive renovations, the Canadian National Vimy Memorial is rededicated by Queen Elizabeth II, 90 years after the Battle of Vimy Ridge.

2010

February 18

John Henry Foster "Jack" Babcock dies at age 109; he is the last known surviving veteran of the Canadian military to have served in the First World War.

RESOURCES

BOOKS

Bennett, Captain S.G. *Regimental History of the 4th Canadian Mounted Rifles.* Toronto: Murray Print Co., 1926.

Christy, N.M. *Gas Attack! The Canadians at Ypres, 1915.* Access to History: The Canadian History Series: No. 1. Nepean, ON: CEF Books, 2002.

Christy, Norm. *Futility and Sacrifice: The Canadians on the Somme, 1916.* Access to History: Canadian History Series: No. 2. Nepean, ON: CEF Books, 2004.

Currie, Arthur. *The Selected Papers of Sir Arthur Currie: Diaries, Letters, and Report to the Ministry, 1917–1933.* Edited by Mark Osborne Humphries. Waterloo, ON: LCMSDS Press of Wilfred Laurier University, 2008.

Gilbert, Adrian. *Going to War in World War I.* London: Franklin Watts, 2001.

Gilbert, Martin. *The Battle of the Somme: The Heroism and Horror of War.* Toronto: McClelland & Stewart, 2006.

Griffith, Paddy. *Fortifications of the Western Front 1914–18.* Oxford: Osprey Publishing, 2004.

Johnston, James Robert. *Riding into War: The Memoir of a Horse Transport Driver 1916–1919.* Fredericton, NB: Goose Lane Editions and the New Brunswick Military Heritage Project, Volume 4, 1971.

McCarthy, Chris. *The Somme: The Day-By-Day Account.* London: Brockhampton Press, 1998.

Middlebrook, Martin. *The First Day on the Somme: 1 July 1916.* Harmondsworth, Middlesex, England: Penguin Books, 1984.

Nicholson, Colonel G.W.L. *Canadian Expeditionary Force 1914–1919: The Official History of the Canadian Army in the First World War.* Ottawa: Queen's Printer and Controller of Stationery, 1962.

Razac, Olivier (translated by Jonathan Kneight). *Barbed Wire: A Political History.* New York: The New Press, 2002.

Ross, Stewart. *The Battle of the Somme.* Chicago: Raintree Press, 2004.

Tyler, G.C.A. *The Lion Rampant: A Pictorial History of the Queen's Own Cameron Highlanders of Canada 1910–1985.* Winnipeg: Public Press, 1985.

WEBSITES

Canadian War Museum: *www.warmuseum.ca.*

Library and Archives Canada (LAC), Lest We Forget Project: *www.collectionscanada.gc.ca/cenotaph/index-e.html.*

LAC, Military and Peacekeeping *www.collectionscanada.gc.ca/military-peace/index-e.html.*

Spartacus Educational, "The Somme": *www.spartacus.schoolnet.co.uk/FWWsomme.htm.*

Veterans Affairs Canada: *www.veterans.gc.ca.*

HOLD THE OXO!

INDEX

Africa, role in First World War, 29, 101, 105
Aircraft, 72, 74–75, 130
Albert, France, 94, 97
Allies, 51, 92, 99, 101, 104
Attestation papers, 22, 28
Australia, role in First World War, 92, 100, 133

Bairnsfather, Bruce (cartoonist), 73, 84
Barbed wire, 43, 54, 58, 63–65, 67, 75, 76, 94, 101, 102
Bayonets, 39, 42, 45, 55, 68
Belgium, 49, 51, 100, 125
Belmont, Manitoba, 19, 15, 117
Bluebirds, 107–09
Borden, Sir Robert, 39, 109
Bramshott, England, 45, 47
Bramshott Military Camp, 47
Bread, shortage, 57, 99–100

"Brooding Soldier" (*see* St. Julien Memorial)
Burials (*see also* Unknown soldier, Casualties), 47, 102–03, 105, 120

Cameron Highlanders, 12, 29, 86, 98
Canada
    conscription, 108–09, 132
    role in the First World War, 27–29, 100, 104, 107
    unrest at home, 57, 82, 132
    voting, 107–09
Canadian 1st Division, 66–67, 104
Canadian National Vimy Memorial (*see* Vimy Memorial)
Canadian Nursing Sisters (*see* Bluebirds)
Canadian Pacific Railway (CPR), 35
Canadian Scottish Battalion, 102
Carrier pigeons, 73, 74, 92
Casualties, 51, 56, 94, 100–01, 103, 104, 131

Casualty Clearing Stations (CCSs), 91, 94, 104, 108

Chlorine (*see* Poison gas)

Christmas truce, 55, 129, 131

Churchill, Winston, 95

Clay-kickers, 54, 55

Cloth Hall, Ypres (*see* Halles of Ypres)

Conscription Crisis, 132

Creeping barrage, 104

Diary entries, 45, 81, 86–87, 97–98

"Ditch of Memory" (*see* Regina Trench)

Dominion Elections Act of 1906, 107

Duckboards, 54, 56, 77

Dugouts, 57, 77, 86–87, 93

"Dulce et Decorum est," 71–72

Enfield rifle (*see* Lee Enfield rifle)

English Channel, 49, 89

Étaples, France, 104, 108, 120

Fargey, Aileen (sister), 32, 40, 58

Fargey, Cecil (brother), 32, 40, 83, 96

Fargey, Frank (brother), 32, 38–40, 79, 81–82

Fargey, Jim

    age, 22

    death, 113–16, 120

    enlistment, 29

    home and family, 31–32, 81–82, 83, 96, 102, 116

    in the trenches, 81–83, 86–87, 96, 97–100

    photos, 32, 33, 41, 46, 115

    training, 38–40, 45

    wounded, 103–04, 111–13

Fargey, Mrs. J., 24, 31–34, 126

Farming, 37, 79, 83, 96

Ferdinand, Franz, 27

First World War Battles

    Amiens, 133

    Flers-Courcelette, 75

    Mount Sorrel, 86

    Passchendaele (Third Battle of Ypres), 87, 103, 132

    Somme, the (First), 75–76, 89–105, 121, 131

    Somme, the (Second), 132

    Verdun, 89, 92, 104, 131

    Vimy Ridge, 21, 104, 132

    Ypres (First), 51, 129

    Ypres (Second), 24, 51, 66–69, 130

    Ypres (Third) (*see* Passchendaele)

Fokker monoplane, 74

"Fokker Scourge," 74, 130

Food in the field (*see also* Rations, Iron rations), 43, 57, 92, 99–100, 112

"Funk holes" (*see* Dugouts)

Gas (*see* Poison gas)
Gas attacks, 51, 66–70, 71–72
Glidden, J.F., 63–64
Gordon, Charles W., 83, 100, 119–21
"Grey-backs" (*see* Lice)

Halles of Ypres, 49, 50, 51, 67
Hitler, Adolf, 91, 131
Horses, 62, 91
Hot air balloons, 72–73
Hughes, Sam (*see also* Ross rifle,
    MacAdam shield-shovels), 39, 44

Influenza, 47
Iron rations, 43

Johnston, James Robert, 38

"Khaki election," 108
Kickers (*see* Clay-kickers)
Kilts, regimental, 39–40, 80, 95–96
Kipling, Rudyard, 123–25
Kitchener's Woods, 68

Laurier, Sir Wilfrid, 108
Le Havre, France, 45
Lee Enfield rifle, 39, 42, 79, 83–85
Lice, 54, 81–82, 108
London, England, 27, 55, 130, 132

MacAdam shield-shovels, 44
Marching, 40, 54, 79, 87, 97, 98, 117
McCrae, John, 24, 130, 132
Menin Gate, 123, 125
Messines, Belgium, 47, 51, 53, 87
Military Voters Act, 109
"Moles," 91
Money, George, 40, 115
Mud (*see also* Weather conditions), 39, 42,
    43, 54, 56, 75, 79, 95–96, 103, 105, 131
Mustard gas (*see also* Poison Gas), 67

Neuve Chapelle, France, 130
Newfoundland Regiment, 95, 100
New Zealand, casualties in First World
    War, 100
No man's land, 54–55, 58, 64, 91, 94–95,
    98, 101
North Sea, 54

"Old Sam Hughes" (*see* Ross rifle)
"Over the top" orders (*see also* No man's
    land), 42, 64, 94, 102

Packs, 40, 44, 80
Passchendaele (*see* First World War Battles)
Pay (soldiers'), 36–37, 53–54, 96
Phosgene (*see also* Poison gas), 67
Pitcairn Craig, W. (Chaplain), 114, 116–17

Poetry of war (*see* War poetry)
Poison gas (*see* also Mustard gas,
     Phosgene), 51, 66–72
Princess Patricia's Canadian Light
     Infantry (PPCLI), 86

"Race to the sea," 49
Rations, 43, 57, 99
Rats, 54, 108
Red River Colony, 36
Regina Trench, 96, 99, 101, 103
Ross rifle, 39, 42, 79
Royal Air Force (RAF), 75
Royal Canadian Army Medical Corp (*see*
     also Bluebirds), 107–08
Royal Flying Corps (RFC), 74, 75

Sadleir, Angela M. (Staff Nurse), 111–14
Salient (*see also* Ypres Salient), 47, 49–51,
     66–68, 95, 97, 123
Sappers, 54, 55, 87
Second World War, 76, 91
Socks, 44, 56, 80
Somme, the (*see* First World War battles)
South Africa, role in First World War,
     101, 105
St. Julien, 68
St. Julien Memorial, 69
Statute of Westminster, 27

Tank warfare, 75–76, 97, 130, 131
Thiepval, 75, 98, 131
Thiepval Memorial to the Missing, 105, 123
Trench foot, 56
Trench runners, 91, 92
Trench warfare, 39, 42, 102–03
Trenches, conditions in, 40, 43, 53–62,
     77–79, 81–83, 85, 96, 98, 103

U-boats, 49, 107
Unknown soldier (*see also* Burial on the
     battlefield), 102–03, 123–25
United States of America, 100, 129, 132

Verdun, 89, 92, 104
Vimy, France, 60, 61
Vimy Memorial, 21, 133

War poetry, 24, 71–72, 85, 123, 127–28
Wartime Elections Act, 108, 109
Weather conditions (*see also* Mud), 40,
     53, 57, 80, 87, 95–96, 98, 99, 101,
     103–04, 131
Western Front, 51, 54, 56, 99
Winnipeg, Manitoba, 29, 57, 82
Wirers, wire-cutters, 57, 65
Women
     role of in war, 48, 107–09
     voting, 107–09

Woods, "Mac," 53, 54, 57, 79, 98, 117–18

YMCA, 82–83
Ypres, 49–51, 55, 66–67, 70, 85, 103, 125
Ypres Salient, 47, 49–51, 66, 69, 95–97, 123

Zeppelins, 39, 130
Zollern Graben Trench, 98, 99

IN THE SAME SERIES

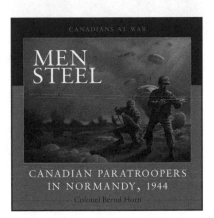

Men of Steel
Canadian Paratroopers in Normandy, 1944
Colonel Bernd Horn
978-1554887088
$19.99

Men of Steel is the gripping story of some of Canada's toughest and most daring soldiers in the Second World War and what they did in their finest hours. Through the lens of these gallant paratroopers, we glimpse the chaos and destruction of combat in the greatest invasion in military history.

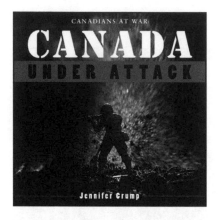

Canada Under Attack
Jennifer Crump
978-1554887316
$19.99

Canadians have been celebrated participants in many conflicts on foreign soils, but most Canadians aren't aware that they've also had to defend themselves at home. Jennifer Crump brings to life the battles fought by Canadians to ensure the country's independence and reveals the invasion plans by the United States and Germany to conquer Canada.

Day of the Flying Fox
The True Story of World War II Pilot Charlie Fox
Steve Pitt
978-1550028089
$19.99

Canadian World War II pilot Charley Fox had a thrilling life, especially on the day in July 1944 when he spotted a black staff car, the kind usually employed to drive high-ranking Third Reich dignitaries. Already noted for his skill in dive-bombing and strafing the enemy, Fox went in to attack the automobile. As it turned out, the car contained famed German General Erwin Rommel, the Desert Fox, and Charley succeeded in wounding him.

Author Steve Pitt focuses on this seminal event in Charley Fox's life and in the war, but he also provides fascinating aspects of the period, including profiles of noted ace pilots Buzz Beurling and Billy Bishop, Jr., and Great Escape architect Walter Floody, as well as sidebars about Hurricanes, Spitfires, and Messerschmitts.

Available at your favourite bookseller.

DUNDURN
www.dundurn.com

What did you think of this book?
Visit www.dundurn.com for reviews, videos, updates, and more!

Marquis Book Printing Inc.

Québec, Canada
2011